FÉNELON

FÉNELON

FÉNELON

A STUDY

by

J. LEWIS MAY

LONDON
BURNS OATES & WASHBOURNE LTD
PUBLISHERS TO THE HOLY SEE

NIHIL OBSTAT:
GEORGIUS CAN. SMITH, S.TH.D., PH.D.,
Censor deputatus.

IMPRIMATUR:
LEONELLUS CAN. EVANS,
Vic. Gen.

MADE AND PRINTED IN GREAT BRITAIN
FOR
BURNS OATES & WASHBOURNE LTD
1938

PREFACE

TO those who are learned in Fénelon and his times, this book will offer nothing new. They will, indeed, find many gaps in it. But it was not for them that I intended it. I wrote it rather for those to whom Fénelon is little more than a name, little more than a vague legend, as for a long time he was to me—vague, but for some mysterious reason, singularly attractive.

It seemed to me—it must have been whispered in my inward ear—that I should find in him the type and exemplar of all that is noblest and most gracious in the genius of France, of France the most civilised of all nations, of France the protectress of the arts and of humane letters. I suspected, in a word, that I should find in him, not only a pattern of all the Christian virtues, but a great scholar and a great gentleman, the shining adornment of an age among the most brilliant that the world has ever known.

True, I had little enough on which to base these intuitions : a couple of sentences from *Télémaque— Calypso ne pouvait se consoler du départ d'Ulysse. Dans sa douleur, elle se trouvait malheureuse d'être immortelle*—which I had got from a very old and courteous gentleman who used to visit my father's house, bringing with him, in his beautiful, old-fashioned, rather fastidious manners, the fragrance of a vanished world—those sentences, and his ' legend,' a few odds and ends of information gathered here and there, and, later on, Pater's account of him in his *Imaginary Portrait* of Antony Watteau.

v

Those opening sentences from *Télémaque* have a notable grace about them. Time was when not to have known them by heart would have been looked on as the mark of a neglected education. It would have been almost as bad as not knowing, *Tityre, tu patulae* . . . or *O fortunatos* . . . Now, I suppose, one may avow one's ignorance of all such things without a blush.

As for Madame Guyon and the Quietists, I confess I found myself in rather deep waters. On the whole I am inclined to doubt whether mysticism takes kindly to our Anglo-Saxon soil. Most of my countrymen would, I think, have sided with Bossuet in that great controversy, and no one was ever less of a mystic than Bossuet. It does not follow that my countrymen would have been right. There is a large admixture of what Matthew Arnold called Philistinism in the average Anglo-Saxon temperament, and Philistinism is apt to bungle the finer issues, when it does not miss them altogether. My own mystical experiences are humble, and I will not enter into them. Such as they are, however, they have made me the liege-man of Fénelon. His own misfortunes, so nobly and submissively borne, confirmed me in that allegiance.

Again, I divined that in Fénelon, the ' Swan of Cambrai,' I should find a votary and a kindred spirit of Virgil. I was not deceived. It gave me what I am afraid is rather an uncharitable satisfaction to hear him say, as he says in his *Letter to the Academy* : ' Woe unto those who thrill not to the beauty of such a line as,

Fortunate senex, hic inter flumina nota . . .'

There are plenty who are deaf to that music to-day. I have enlarged on the communion of spirit between Virgil and Fénelon in the pages which follow, and I need not dwell upon it here.

There was yet another thing which I looked to find in Fénelon, and here, too, my expectations were abundantly fulfilled. I looked to find in him, *mutatis mutandis*, a counterpart, a *pendant* to Newman. As I say, I was not disappointed. In their general attitude towards such things as the fine-arts, literature, education, worldly society; in their common love of naturalness and simplicity; in their joint dislike of anything that savoured of pompousness, or pretence, or pose; even in such details as their preference for Classical architecture over Gothic, their points of resemblance are as numerous as they are remarkable. I am, of course, speaking of them, not as theologians—that, I am scarcely competent to do—but as humanists. As such, their position is unassailable. To frequent their society, to listen to their discourse—for their voices still live in the written word—is in very truth a liberal education. 'The Church,' says Janet, 'may have found in Bossuet a stronger bulwark against peril, but what an ornament she would have lacked if Fénelon had never lived!'

J. L. M.

CONTENTS

LIST OF ILLUSTRATIONS

FÉNELON

CHAPTER I

THE CHILD IN THE CHÂTEAU

NO name falls more musically on the ear, or awakens more stirring memories of the past than that of Périgord. Nowhere, throughout the length and breadth of France, are the aspects of nature more romantic or more varied—rolling stretches of heath and moorland, vine-clad hills where the grape ripens gently in the glow of a hot but not intemperate sun, lonely glens and dark ravines along whose narrow channel, foaming and flashing over rock and boulder, the torrent hastens to the plain ; and then, in sudden contrast to these wild and desolate scenes, you will come, as you descend towards the valleys, upon a pastoral land, a smiling land of plenty, where the air is bland and the hills take on a softer curve. Here, in the lowlands, the soil is rich and loamy, bringing forth in their due season all the kindly fruits of the earth. In the spring, the panorama is diversified by myriads of fruit trees in all the glory of their blossoming, and, so equable and benignant is the climate, the blossom never belies its vernal promise.

To all these natural beauties of the land must be added its heroic and legendary past. No region brings out into stronger relief the chain which binds the long succession of generations one to another. Primeval man chose it for his dwelling place. The

caves of its valleys, its vast limestone terraces,
beheld the first hunters, the first warriors, and the
first artists. The discoveries made in Dordogne,
particularly at Eyzies, throw a valuable light on the
characteristics and mode of life of the remotest
ancestors of the human race. From one millenary to
another, each succeeding epoch has left its distinctive
trace upon the province.

It was in the heart of *le Périgord Noir*—Black
Périgord—so called, perhaps, from its rugged aspect,
its shadowy forests, its dark, mysterious glens and
combes—in *le Sarladais*, at the ancestral château of
his race, that, on August 6 in the year 1651, François
de Salignac de la Mothe-Fénelon first saw the light.
Three years earlier, in 1648, the Treaty of West-
phalia had at last brought the Thirty Years' War to
a close. Little more than a year later, Bossuet, at
first the friend of Fénelon, and afterwards his bitter
and relentless foe, was ordained to the priesthood.
One other date is deserving of mention : in the year
1647 was born, at Montargis, Jeanne Marie
Bouvières de la Mothe, afterwards Madame Guyon,
who was to play so striking and so disastrous a part
in Fénelon's career.

When, however, we speak of the birthplace of
Fénelon and say that he was born at the château of
that name, the matter is not quite so simple as it
might seem, for there are, or rather were, in the
same district, three châteaux, which, with varying
degrees of plausibility, compete for the honour.

In the first place, there is the Château de Salignac
(commonly, but erroneously, called the Château de
Salignac-Fénelon) in the Commune de Salignac,
some ten miles distant from the historic town of
Sarlat. The See of Sarlat, which was then occupied
by an uncle of Fénelon's, was merged, in later years,
with that of Périgueux, whose bishops now style
themselves ' Evêques de Périgueux et de Sarlat.'

Secondly, there was, at La Mothe Fénelon, a little commune in the arrondissement of Gourdon, another château of which no trace now remains.

Lastly, in the Commune of Sainte Mondane, in the district of Sarlat itself, and not more than two or three miles from that town, there still stands a Château de Fénelon which is now universally regarded as the Archbishop's authentic birthplace.

Some hundred yards or so from the château itself is a house to which tradition gives the name of *la maison de la nourrice de Fénelon*, over the door of which is carved the date of his birth, 1651. The same date is inscribed on the lintel of an old dwelling-house in a spot known as ' Le Roc,' about a quarter of a mile away.

In one of the rooms of the château stands a great four-poster with a magnificent canopy, said to be the bed in which Fénelon was born. The greater part of the château dates from the fifteenth century, but there have been many subsequent additions. Originally, the building consisted of no more than a donjon and a *corps-de-garde*, surrounded by a twofold battlemented rampart. It seems to have been erected at the same time, and on the same plan, as a fortress, now in ruins, at Milhac, and as another almost identical structure at Carlux. Two towers of formidable strength and solidity were afterwards added, to be followed still later by two more of lighter construction.

In Louis XIII's day, the Château de Fénelon laid aside something of its war-like aspect. A portion of the façade was demolished, and a terrace with a stone balustrade constructed in its place, above the still existing drawbridge.

There are evidences that a large part of the building on the chapel side, looking to the south, was at some time ravaged by fire, for the stones of the walls there still show scorched and reddened, as by the flames of some fierce and far-off conflagration.

The last member of the Fénelon family to occupy, or rather to own, the château—for he seldom lived in it—was the Archbishop's nephew, ' Fanfan,' the son of one of his half-brothers.

Now this ' Fanfan,' a favourite nephew, to whom Fénelon addressed some of the most delightful of his letters, seems to have been so lightly bound to the ancestral home by ties of sentiment, that he sold it to a M. de Boulhac, or Bouillac, a farmer of taxes, who disposed of it in his turn to the Marquis d'Abzac de la Douze. About the time of the Restoration, the steward of the Marquis, one Pigniez, himself became owner of the château. In 1860, M. Pigniez sold the property to the Marquis de Maleville. By this time it had fallen into a state of complete dilapidation. The roofs were falling in, and one of the bedrooms on the first floor, which was always known as Fénelon's room, was used as a sheep-pen. Thirty years the new owner spent in restoring the château. The work was carried out with great taste and judgement and in such a manner as scrupulously to preserve the marked individuality of the ancient abode. On the death of the Marquis de Maleville, which occurred in 1910, the château became the property of his son, M. Lucien de Maleville, in whose hands it remained until 1927, when it was sold to the Marquis de San Carlos.

The family of Fénelon, which was extremely ancient—its records going back well into the tenth century—was allied with some of the most illustrious houses in the kingdom. Most of its members had been soldiers or diplomats, and had acquitted themselves with credit alike in field and council-chamber. One of Fénelon's great-great uncles, Bertrand de Salignac de Fénelon, was present with the Duc de Guise at the siege of Metz. He was subsequently appointed Ambassador at the Court of Queen Elizabeth. The King having enjoined him to put the best construction he could on the massacre of St. Bartholomew, he met the request with a retort as bold as it was blunt. ' Sire,' said he, ' you should tell that to the people who were responsible for it ! '

Fénelon's father, Pons de Salignac, Comte de la Mothe Fénelon, having been left a widower after his wife had borne him twelve children, married again, taking for his second wife Louise de la Cropte de Saint-Abre by whom he had four more, among them the future Archbishop-Duke of Cambrai.

The family of Fénelon, though old and distinguished, was extremely poor, and Comte Pons must have found it no easy matter to feed and clothe his numerous progeny, to say nothing of educating them in a manner appropriate to their birth and station. It was well that the land was rich and fertile, that the woods about the place abounded in game, and the rivers in fish. With such a considerable family to feed and clothe—to say nothing of servants and retainers—the problem can hardly have been a simple one, and those *res angustae* which, according to Horace, play so salutary a part in the formation of character must have been not a little in evidence at the Château de Fénelon. 'Fénelon,' said Saint-Simon later on, ' was a man of quality without a penny-piece to call his own.'

The fate of the other children, all those brothers and half-brothers, sisters and half-sisters, has for the most part been left unrecorded. One of the half-brothers went out as a missionary to Canada, and died there. Another is said to have been drowned while bathing in the Dordogne at Saint-Julien de Lampon, a village some two miles distant from the Château de Fénelon. Concerning the father, Comte Pons de Fénelon, history is silent. He was a gentleman farmer, or at least he had to lead the life

B

of one, and therefore ' tilth and vineyard, hive, and horse, and herd ' no doubt formed the staple of his preoccupations.

Fénelon's mother, Louise de la Cropte de Saint-Abre, who came of an old and honourable family of Périgord, was still but a young woman when Comte Pons, now well on in years, took her for his second wife. Though she is described as punctual and devout in her religious observances, we may take it with confidence that there was nothing sombre or forbidding about her piety. That she was a good manager we need have no doubt, and she answered, we may be sure, to that pattern of the well-bred woman which her son had in mind when, in his *Traité de l'Éducation des Filles*, he spoke of ' women who, in addition to their natural authority, and their constant presence in the house, have the further advantage of having been born thrifty, attentive to detail, industrious, winning, and persuasive.'

Of the childhood and early adolescence of Fénelon, few details have been preserved. The name and identity of the tutor by whom an enduring love of classical literature and antiquity was early implanted in his heart and mind, are also unknown to us. Whoever that tutor was, he must have been a man in whom sound learning was united with great tact and charm in the imparting of it. His ferule was gentle, yet not too indulgent. If we may judge by the tastes afterwards exhibited by his pupil, he was something of a bibliophile, to whom a well-printed page or an elegant binding was by no means a matter of indifference. That this tutor had a fine literary taste, an insight that penetrated beyond the mere letter of the things he taught, we may infer from the degree in which these qualities enriched the mind of his pupil. The spirit that breathes in the *Letter to the Academy* is acquired young, or not at all. The tutor did not sow his seed in vain. It fell on soil of rare fertility, and the flowering was gracious and abundant. If the tutor was fortunate in his pupil, we owe it to the nameless memory of the former to acknowledge that the pupil was fortunate in his tutor. We may picture them, ensconced together in the window-seat of one of the great rooms of the castle, deep in their book— Homer, or Virgil, or Horace—while the logs are blazing on the open hearth ; or seated, on summer days, on a bench in some sheltered nook under the grey walls where the martlet nests beneath the eaves, or pacing side by side in gentle converse along the garden walks, with their borders of brilliant flowers and sweet-scented herbs.

What manner of child was he who was destined to cast such a lustre over his age and country ? Tall, slim, rather delicate-looking he must have been, with big, expressive, dreamy eyes, pale, finely-chiselled features, long sensitive hands, easy and graceful in his movements, with, even now, a touch of command, almost of majesty, in a demeanour at once gracious and remote, courteous and detached, gentle and austere. Too young and too delicate to join in hunting the wolf and the wild boar with his elder brothers and their comrades, he must often have heard the horn of the huntsman echoing in the woods about the castle, and listened of an evening round the fire to the story of the day's run. Wolves are still to be found in Périgord, or at least in the solitudes of the Nontronnais, and even now, when compelled by cold and hunger, they will steal down by night to the farms and attack the watch dog in the yard itself. But in Fénelon's time, when the forests were far more extensive than they are to-day, wolves were a perpetual menace to cattle and to human life. Measures for their systematic exter-mination were obligatory on the inhabitants, and whenever the *lieutenant de la louveterie*, or master of the wolf hounds, gave orders that a hunt was to take place, every able-bodied peasant had to answer the summons in person or by proxy. Sundays and holidays of obligation were chosen for these expeditions in order that the work in the fields should not be interrupted, but, out of regard for the spiritual welfare of the participants, the operations did not begin until after Mass. Armed with staves, pitch-forks, reaping-hooks, and any weapon that came to hand, the mob beat up the quarry in the direction of ' the quality,' who alone were privileged to dispatch it with firearms.

In these wolf-hunts and in the hardly less exciting and perilous pursuit of the boar, Fénelon was too young and too delicate to take part, but he would certainly have heard all about them from his elders. The custom of story-telling, popular in all country places, was a passion with the Périgourdins, and of an evening, by the glowing hearth in the great kitchen while the chestnuts were a-peeling and the women busy at the distaff, the hours would be sped with tales of the denizens of the dim forests, of wolves and wild boars as well as of fairies and gnomes, of beautiful ladies and gallant knights, of dwarfs and witches, of unearthly music and mocking laughter heard among the forest branches, of pixies who, when you pursued them, would suddenly change into a silver birch, or a flashing rivulet, or a bird on the wing. Tales woven of such themes as these would have been poured of an evening, when the light had faded from the sky and the owls were hooting about the castle walls, into ears that in the daytime had drunk in stories of the gods and heroes of ancient Greece or Rome.

Doubtless his mother played an important, though not an obtrusive, part in his education. So fine a nature could scarcely have been produced in an atmosphere in which the feminine graces were of little account. ' My young days,' he tells us, ' were pleasant and unrestrained, taken up with congenial studies and intercourse with delightful friends.' Père de Guerbeuf, one of his eighteenth-century editors, remarks that his upbringing was ' plain, sensible, and soundly Christian.' There was nothing startling or out of the way about it. It was none the worse for that.

As a child, Fénelon was delicate and sensitive, highly strung, quick in his movements as in his understanding, yet a prey at times to that dreaminess and languor which children not infrequently betray when one or both of the parents have married when considerably past their prime. In his *robe*—for in those days, until their first communion, boys and girls were dressed alike—Fénelon, with his slim figure, his gentleness and his graceful manners, must have looked very like a girl.

From his earliest days Fénelon was a spirit destined for the sanctuary. His delicate health, his studious habits, and, not least, the straitened circumstances of his family, were hardly calculated to promise success and rapid advancement in a secular career. But these practical considerations, cogent as they may have been in the eyes of his father and of his uncle, the Bishop, did but set the seal on his own inward vocation to the religious life.

Yet Fénelon's boyhood was not all study, nor was he for ever at home. He was a frequent visitor at his uncle's at Sarlat, and, pretty regularly, he would spend his holidays with his maternal grandparents at their Château de Beauséjour, near Tocane-Saint Abre, on the banks of the Dronne.

Tradition tells of playfellows, boys and girls, and of a love-idyll in which the heroine was a child named Marie de Rocanadel who lived at the château of that name, the ruins of which may still be seen in the Commune de Verignac, a few miles distant from the Château de Fénelon.

Though he took part with zest in games with children of his own age, he was never at a loss, never disconsolate, if left to himself and his own resources. Of him it may indeed be said, *nunquam minus solus quam cum solus*. Always, one imagines, there must have been, notwithstanding the grace and fascination of his ways, something hieratic, something remote and consecrate, something of the *noli me tangere* in his bearing, even to those with whom he was most familiar.

It was, then, as one predestined to be in the world but not of it that he was soon to quit the home, the woods and streams and meadows which he loved so well, and to bid farewell to the tutor who had already implanted in him a taste for letters beyond his years, in order to follow a more definitely ecclesiastical course of study at Cahors. This course was adopted on the advice of his uncle, the Bishop of Sarlat, who, recognising in this fragile flower of a late marriage, a spirit of rare distinction, seems early to have taken him under his special protection. Sarlat, whither the boy must often have gone on a visit to his uncle—it is only two or three miles over the hill from the Château de Fénelon—and over which it seems the Fénelons exercised a sort of suzerainty as being the great family of the district— was a city which prided itself, and with some reason, on its intellectual culture. The citizens held in highest honour there were, not so much the men of wealth or of civic eminence, as in Périgueux, but *les érudits*, scholars, and men devoted to the pursuit of the sciences. This is illustrated by the statement of one Bouquier, a future *conventionnel*, who, in an essay on the respective condition of Périgord and Limousin which he addressed to the National Assembly, sets forth the reasons why the Périgourdins

should be relieved of some of their taxes. 'Périgueux,' he said, ' is inhabited by a crowd of *bourgeois*
who have no thought for anything save their precious
"privileges." Sarlat is devoted to the cultivation
of the mind.' It was therefore becoming, thought
Bouquier, that their burden should be lightened.

A shining example of Sarlat's intellectuals is Jean
Tarde, a canon of the cathedral there, who flourished
some fifty years before Fénelon was born. He was
a man of extraordinary versatility, one to whom no
branch of human knowledge was closed. He knew
Latin, Greek, Hebrew, and was deeply versed in
History, Geography, Mathematics, Astronomy,
Physics, and Theology. In spite of his absorption
in these multifarious occupations, he found time to
make two journeys to Rome. Wherever he halted,
the learned men of the district came in crowds to
greet him, vying with each other for the honour of
offering him hospitality. He kept up a regular
correspondence with Galileo, whom he frequently
visited when he was in Rome. He even published
a monograph for the purpose of proving that
Galileo's theory involved nothing at variance with
religion.

But if they were devoted to the pursuit of learning
and the cultivation of the things of the mind, these
' intellectuals ' were lacking neither in courage nor
resource. The town of Sarlat, surrounded as it is
by rising ground, was not particularly well situated
to withstand a siege, and yet, in 1587, the inhabitants
succeeded in keeping at bay the forces of the
redoubtable Turenne. Three years later, their
coolness and readiness of wit enabled them to rid
themselves of some awkward visitors. One Saturday,
on June 23, 1590, at five o'clock in the afternoon, one
of the most intrepid of the local leaders of the
League, Jean de Vassal, Seigneur de la Tourette, a
former Archdeacon of Sarlat Cathedral, presented

himself at the Porte de la Rigaudie with a company
of fighting men. With the connivance of some men
of Sarlat who favoured their cause, these Leaguers
succeeded in getting into the city without striking
a blow. Four days later, the Consuls gave the
leaders of the League to understand that the
Protestants of Douenne were about to take possession
of the Château de la Boëtie, and they implored them
to go in haste, either to defend it, or to raze it to the
ground, to prevent the enemy from converting it
into a base. The chiefs of the League, quite unsus-
picious of a ruse, sallied forth with the greater
number of their troops, and hurried away at top
speed to demolish the Château de la Boëtie. When
they got back they found the gates of Sarlat closed
and barred against them, and were obliged to depart
‘ shamefaced as foxes who had been taken in by a
parcel of barn-door fowls.’ Then those who had
been left behind in the city were disarmed and
escorted like little children to the gates and gently
told to depart.

The Bishop of Sarlat, if kindly and generous at
heart, seems to have been possessed of a will of his
own. We may picture him as a cultured, energetic,
and capable diocesan who looked for, and doubtless
received, the obedience of all those of whom he
considered himself entitled to expect it, his kinsfolk
no less than his clergy. To this benevolent authori-
tarian Fénelon's mother doubtless applied for advice
in matters connected with the upbringing of her
children and the choosing of their destination in
life. He would have had a decisive voice in the
selection of a tutor for his nephew, and, being a
man of experience and perspicacity, he could scarcely
have failed to discern in this pensive, delicate child,

a spirit of unusual promise. It was no doubt at his instigation that, at the age of twelve, Fénelon was taken away from the domestic circle and sent to the University of Cahors, and thence, some two years later, to the Collège du Plessis in Paris, where he came under the protection of his other uncle, the Marquis de Fénelon, a distinguished soldier and diplomat. The Marquis, in addition to the fame he had won as a soldier and a statesman, was also a man of exalted ideals and profound piety. He belonged to the Company of the Blessed Sacrament, whose mission it was to bring about the moral regeneration of the country, and he was a close friend of M. Olier, the founder of Saint-Sulpice, and of M. Tronson, his successor. Bossuet, then coming into prominence, was among his more intimate acquaintance. The Marquis had lost his only and deeply loved son at the siege of Candia, and all the affection he had formerly bestowed on his own offspring, he henceforth lavished on his nephew. M. Olier was his spiritual director, and it was by his advice that, in 1672 or 1673, when he was about twenty-one or twenty-two, young Fénelon became a student at Saint-Sulpice. He was entered at the *Petit Séminaire*, the section set apart for students of delicate health.

It appears to have been sometime during the year 1675 that Fénelon was ordained, and that the Church was enriched by the accession to the ranks of her clergy of one of her greatest adornments, one in whose character the attributes of the accomplished man of the world, versed in all the graces of fashionable society are found united with the mystical ardours of the saint and the fervour of an exalted piety.

Fénelon, then, after two years or so at the Collège du Plessis, entered the Seminary of Saint-Sulpice, where he pursued his theological studies under the

direction of M. Tronson, for whom he then conceived, and ever afterwards retained, the profoundest
affection.

 ' How dearly I should love,' he says in a letter to
his uncle, the Marquis de Fénelon, ' to give you some
detailed account of my relations with M. Tronson;
but of a truth I hardly know what to tell you ; for,
perfectly free and open-hearted as I take myself to
be towards you, I nevertheless avow, and I know
you will not be jealous, that I am even more so
towards M. Tronson, and I should find it extremely
difficult to give you an idea how completely I am at
one with him.' And how completely M. Tronson
read the heart of his pupil will presently appear.

CHAPTER II

THE CATECHIST

AS soon as he had taken orders, Fénelon was assigned some work in the parish of Saint-Sulpice, labouring in the slums there, toiling with unwearying ardour to illumine the lives of the unhappy, the vicious, and the oppressed with the light of faith and hope. He also gave religious instruction to children. His work as a catechist was singularly successful, and his mode of teaching possessed a charm, a grace, and a persuasiveness that had their effect on a far wider audience than the children for whom they were primarily intended. Men and women of the fashionable world flocked to see and hear this young priest, whose bearing was at once so gentle and so noble, and whose words, uttered in a voice of singular sweetness, had such marvellous power to charm and to persuade.

His success as a catechist, however, did not prevent him from endeavouring to secure a position offering a wider scope for his talents. There is a letter dated 1674, addressed to his uncle the Bishop, in which he intimates his desire to get himself elected delegate for Bordeaux at the Clerical Assembly to be held the following year. The bishops, it appears, had sworn not to allow themselves to be canvassed. This, however, did not prevent my lord of Sarlat from begging the support of his colleague of Saintes, whereupon the latter reproached him for his non-observance of the rules about canvassing. The candidate then requested his other uncle, the

Marquis, to intervene with the Bishop of Saintes, who, it turned out, was himself as much of a transgressor as the Bishop of Sarlat.

'There is no doubt,' wrote Fénelon, ' that M. de Saintes makes himself out a great deal more scrupulous than he really is ; for at the very time he was indulging in these reproaches, he was secretly supporting the candidature of the Abbé de Saint Luc, who told me so himself. Without breaking any rules, it was quite allowable for M. de Sarlat to tell the Bishops that I intended to stand and to explain the reasons which might lead them to support me. . . .' All of which shows him to be a young man by no means indifferent to his own temporal advancement. The election does not seem to have gone in his favour, despite the energy displayed in his behalf by his family.

It was now that he began to dream of foreign missions. One of his half-brothers, who had preceded him at Saint-Sulpice, had gone as a missionary to Canada, where he was fated to leave his bones. Fénelon, it seems, wanted to follow in his steps, but the project was vetoed by his uncle, the Bishop. How could a young man of such delicate constitution dream of facing the hardships of a Canadian winter ? It was madness to think of it. The idea was abandoned, but not the hope of distinguishing himself in the missionary field. If Canada was denied him, then why should not Asia Minor, the Levant, and especially Greece afford a theatre for his evangelising zeal ?

In 1679 he went on a visit to his uncle at Sarlat and gazed once again upon the scenes of his childhood. It was when his sojourn there was drawing to a close that he wrote in the following strain, it is supposed, to Bossuet. The letter is highly characteristic :

'A number of little things have been occurring, one after another, to delay my return to Paris ; but at last, Monseigneur, I am starting. I feel almost as if I could fly. With this journey in front of me, my thoughts have been dwelling on one longer still. The whole of Greece lies open before me. The Sultan shrinks back in terror. Already the Peloponesus is breathing the air of freedom, and the Church of Corinth is about to put forth new bloom. The voice of the Apostle shall again be heard in the land. I feel as though I had been wafted on wings to those noble scenes and priceless ruins, there to refresh my soul, not only with the sight of those wondrous buildings, but to bathe it in the very spirit of antiquity. I turn my steps towards the Areopagus where, to the sages of the world, St. Paul proclaimed the advent of the Unknown God. But after the sacred comes the profane, and I do not forget to make my way down to the Piræus, where Socrates is busily engaged planning the scheme of his ideal Republic. I scale the twin peaks of Parnassus and cull the laurels of Delphi, I revel in the delights of Tempe. When shall the blood of the Turks mingle with the blood of the Persians on the plains of Marathon, so that the whole of Greece may be given up to religion, philosophy, and the fine arts, which look upon her as their native home ?

>   . . . . Arva, beata
> Petamus arva, divites et insulas.

I shall not forget thee, O Isle made sacred by the heavenly visions of the beloved disciple ! O happy Patmos, I shall go and, on thy soil, kiss the very ground whereon the apostle trod, and I shall seem to behold the heavens opening above me. My bosom will swell with indignation against the false prophet who was fain to take it upon himself to unfold the oracles of the true one, and I shall bless the Almighty for that He, far from casting down the Church in a fall like Babylon's, flung chains about the dragon, and gave her the victory. Already I see the end of the Great Schism and the reuniting of East and West. Asia I behold, the sound of her sighs reaching even to the banks of the Euphrates, seeing the day dawn again, when the long night is past ; the land hallowed by the Saviour's steps and watered with His Blood, set free from its desecrators and clothed in fresh glory ; lastly, the children of Abraham, scattered over the face of the earth, more numerous than the stars in heaven, who, gathered together from the four corners of the world, shall come in their hosts to acknowledge the Christ whom they pierced. But enough, Monseigneur ; I will desist. You will be relieved to hear that this is my last letter and my final outburst of enthusiasm, for you may be finding it rather importunate. Pray excuse it as eloquent of my longing to converse with you from afar, ere yet I can do so face to face.'

This letter, which has been blamed in some quarters for its alleged flippancy, deserves to be studied with some attention, for it shows how, in Fénelon, a love for the intellectual graces, the adornments of the mind, co-existed with the profoundest piety, the liveliest apprehension of the reality and the nearness of things unseen. There is in Fénelon, despite his deep religious sense, a *quelquechose de mondain et de terrestre*, a hint that he did not disdain the art of social life, which recalls the portrait drawn by Renan of M. de Guelen, the

Archbishop of Paris who appointed Dupanloup as superior of the Seminary of Saint-Nicholas du Chardonnet. 'I well remember,' says Renan in his *Souvenirs d'Enfance et de Jeunesse*, 'his beautiful countenance (it was an almost feminine beauty), his graceful figure, the fascinating elegance of his every movement. His mind was furnished exclusively with the sort of culture that sits so delightfully on a thoroughly well-bred man of the world. Religion, as he understood it, was inseparable from good manners and the sweet reasonableness that comes of a classical education.' And with Dupanloup, too, Fénelon has some points of resemblance, with Dupanloup who, according to Renan, looked upon Virgil as at least of equal importance with the Gospel in the education of a priest, and whose favourite quotation from the Bible was *Da mihi animas, cetera tolle tibi*, 'because it ended like a pentameter.' But the truest parallel of all would be Newman, who, though of no ascertainable nobility of lineage, was yet endowed with that indefinable aristocracy of the spirit which gave him—which gives every man so endowed—the unquestioning and enthusiastic allegiance of his fellows. 'There is,' observes Lord Haldane, 'always some kind of uniqueness in the men whom the world distinguishes as leaders, something that appeals to the imagination. No man is great merely because he preaches a particular doctrine. Whether it be in his deeds, or in his words, or in his writing, what moves those who follow him is what is beyond his mere doctrine, that in him which fires the imagination and makes others feel that in him there is what cannot be adequately described or forecast. He is for them an individual marked out from the others around him by a quality that cannot be exhausted in any phrases.' But in Fénelon, as in Newman, this fascination, this mysterious power, being innate and not acquired, given not sought, was not inconsistent with an entire humility in its possessor, an utter meekness, yet a meekness so interfused with dignity that violence is disarmed by it, and stubbornness put to shame. It is then with Newman once more, Newman whom the writer just quoted calls ' one of the great Humanists of English literature, a man with an almost matchless sense both of form and of reality,' that Fénelon invites comparison, with Newman who has sung the praises of Athens in words that soar on wings of gold and azure ; with Newman who coached his schoolboys in the acting of Terence and proved himself a born ' producer ' ; with Newman, whose love of classical literature in general and of Virgil in particular, inspired some of his most exquisite and deeply moving prose. Yet, despite the charm and fascination of their speech and bearing, despite the indefinable magnetism which drew men irresistibly to their allegiance—a charm and fascination and a magnetism which continue to lay their spell on successive generations—despite all this, there was in both a certain barrier, on the hither side of intimacy, beyond which none might penetrate, and beyond which one divined uplands, cold, austere, remote, and an air too rarefied for ordinary folk to breathe.

It is worth while to notice, in passing, that Newman, too, as a young man, was fired by the missionary zeal. ' I think,' he says in the autobiographical fragment that has come down to us, ' I shall either die within college walls, or as a missionary in a foreign land. No matter where, so that I die in Christ.'

For a time, after his ordination, Fénelon acted as Superior of the *Nouvelles Catholiques*, a community founded in 1634 by Archbishop Gondi in order to instruct and confirm in the Faith women newly converted from Protestantism. Fénelon's gifts

eminently fitted him for such a post and he fulfilled
his duties with singular success.

In the year 1681, Fénelon, who was then thirty
years of age, became Prior of Carennac, his uncle
the Bishop of Sarlat having resigned that benefice in
his favour. The priory was a sort of fief, or family
possession, of the Fénelons. The first member of
the family to become Dean of Carennac was Louis,
the son of François de Salignac and Marie de
Bouneval, who was made Dean at the age of eleven
by a Bull of Pope Paul V. He died in 1630, shortly
after being ordained priest. The benefice then
passed to his brother François, a doctor of the
Sorbonne, who had already acquired a reputation as
a theologian. From 1655 onwards, he held it in
conjunction with the bishopric of Sarlat which was,
as it were, an ecclesiastical appanage of the family.

Fénelon was greatly pleased at receiving such a
token of his uncle's goodwill, for it added, not
inconsiderably, alike to his dignity and his income.
His satisfaction is vividly reflected in a letter he wrote
to his cousin-german, Marie-Thérèse Françoise,
Marquise de Laval, in which he gives her a charming
and gently ironic description of the ceremonies
which accompanied his arrival at Carennac when he
went thither to assume the office of Prior. The
letter, brimming over with gaiety and lively humour,
is famous, and every book dealing with Fénelon
quotes it, or at least long extracts from it. The
present parish-priest of Carennac has even conceived
the happy idea of selling illustrated reprints of it to
visitors, the proceeds going towards the upkeep of
his church, a singularly beautiful one. Nevertheless,
familiar as it is, the letter is at once so characteristic,
and so charming that to omit it would be like the
wilful withholding from his portrait of a revealing
ray of light.

It was the spring-time of the year—the letter is

c

dated May 22, 1681—and the pathway of the future seemed strewn with flowers.

'Aye, Madame,' he says, 'have no doubt about it; I am a man destined to come on the scene with pomp and circumstance. You remember the magnificent reception your folk at Bellac gave me. Well, I'm now going to tell you how I have been honoured here. M. de Rouffillac, as representing the nobility; M. Bosc, the Curé, on behalf of the clergy; M. Rigaudie, the Prior, for the monastic body; and, finally, the local farmers, for the rest of the population, came all the way to Sarlat to offer me their greetings. And so I set forth in majesty, encompassed about by all these representatives. And now behold me at the port of Carennac, the whole population packed in a dense crowd on the quay. Two boats, with the *élite* of the citizens on board, advance towards me and then it is I notice that, by a brave device, the doughtiest troops of the district are hidden away in a corner of the beautiful island you know so well. Thence they advance to greet me, marching in battle array, with much letting off of muskets. Instantly the air is darkened with smoke from all this firing, and nought is heard save alarming explosions of gunpowder. The mettlesome steed I was bestriding was for plunging into the river, but I, less enterprising than he, took my stand on *terra firma*. Then to the rattle of musketry is added the roll of the drums. I cross the lovely Dordogne, which you can hardly see for the boats that are escorting mine. On shore a a group of monks await me with grave and venerable mien. Their address is filled with the loftiest encomiums. My reply is suave and gentle, but not without a touch of the sublime.

The vast throng divides to yield me a passage through their midst. Everyone scans me with searching eyes if haply he may read in mine what destiny awaits him. In this wise, I make my way up towards the castle with slow and measured tread, so that I may offer myself yet a little longer to the inquisitive inspection of the public.

Meanwhile, from innumerable throats goes up the joyous shout: " He'll be the apple of our eye ! "

And now behold me at the Priory gates ! The consuls address me through their mouth-piece, the Orator-Royal. That will tell you in what stately gems of eloquence, what rhetorical flights, the speech abounded. They liken me to the Sun. Anon, I am the Moon. Thereafter all the brightest stars have the honour of resembling me. From the stars we come to the elements, and thence to the meteors, and we finish up in happy style with the creation of the world. By this time the sun had gone to bed, and to set the seal on the likeness between us, I retired to my room, and made ready to follow his example.'

A few days later, he followed up this letter with another, in a similar vein, to the same correspondent :

' I went through Sarlat . . . stopping there one day because the local Ciceros were to argue a big case and I wanted to hear them. Needless to say, these learned gentlemen started with the Creation of the world and went on straight through the Flood, till they got to the matter in hand. The question at issue was whether bread was to be distributed to some children who had no bread to eat. Oh, what a strange twist of Fortune ! The advocate got plenty of praise ; but the children got no bread. The hearing was adjourned ; that is lawyer's jargon for telling the unlucky creatures that they'd have to plead on an empty stomach. That much having been settled, the judges gravely got up and went to lunch. I did likewise.'

He loved Carennac. Its image never faded from his heart. It is indeed a delightful place. After foaming and swirling through deep and narrow channels among the mountains of Auvergne and the lonely heights of Limousin, the Dordogne reaches Quercy, and suddenly its valley opens out, its banks become less steep. All along, from Argentat to Beaulieu, the river winds through dark ravines and savage vales whose precipitous cliffs are shadowed by sombre woods of holm-oak and chestnut. But at Beaulieu the country grows more pastoral, more kindly in its aspect. Lovingly the little town looks down upon the image of its quaint dwellings, its broad-spreading plane-trees, its delicious little chapel, mirrored in the placid water of the river. Henceforth it is through smiling lands that, silently and softly, the Dordogne flows on to join its sister stream, the Cere. Not far from Bretenoux, a half-ruined but still beautiful memorial of the warlike past, the two rivers mingle their waters, lately so wild and turbulent, in soft and peaceful unison. They broaden out in the fertile plain that girdles in the heights of Castelnau, crowned with its grim red ruins. Then again the river divides to fold in its embrace a line of long, green islands where, behind a fringe of willows, rich meadows bare their bosom to the sky. Still more open the country grows, the horizon still more distant. The Dordogne, which in its earlier course has beheld so many wild and desolate scenes, seems to grow indolent beneath the caress of blander skies, as it flows gently on by smiling fields and happy villages. Of those happy villages, Carennac is one of the pleasantest. Its old, white houses, ' with the gadding vine o'ergrown,' hurrying down the steep hillside seem to have been stayed, as by enchantment, on the river's brink. Stalwart, four square to all the winds of heaven, an ancient Norman tower rises up from a medley of peaceful, mellow-tinted roofs. A little château gazes down from its delicate mullioned windows to the shady walk beneath, where the townsfolk came at evening, the day's work done, to refresh their spirits and feast their eyes on the softly-flowing, poplar-shaded river.

The château, the church, a tower and a few buildings are all that remains of the former Cluniac priory which, according to tradition, was founded by St. Odilo in the eleventh century. Fénelon, after his presentation, resided at the Priory from time to time. An island in the Dordogne, facing the Priory, bears the name of Calypso, and one of the towers has been christened *Télémaque*. Against all probability, the tradition persists that here it was that Fénelon wrote a portion of his *Télémaque*.

The Dordogne, the rugged, barren heights of its source, the rich pastoral scenes of its middle course, the homeless ocean into which it flows at last, might be taken as a symbol of Fénelon's own life—his childhood nurtured amid the austere, yet kindly, surroundings of a noble but impoverished house ; next smiled upon by Fortune that seemed to promise every gift and distinction to which noble birth and genius might aspire ; cheated of this fair guerdon and fated to end his days in exile from the Court of which at one time he promised to be so brilliant an adornment. Was this disaster ? Surely not. ' Death lays his icy hand on Kings ! ' The radiance of the

'*roi soleil*' has grown more than a little tarnished.
The demi-god has shrunk to very small dimensions,
a shred of dim brocade, a piece of bric-à-brac, a
curio, pitiable and a little comic, who once went
clothed in majesty while the trumpets blared and the
cymbals clashed. But the figure of Fénelon,
solitary, stately, forlorn, stands out in clear, unfading
relief. Should we remember him, as now we do, or
venerate, or love him, merely as the favourite of
Kings and Princes, or the spiritual confidant, the
fashionable confessor, of noble lords and perfumed
ladies of the Court, flattered and favoured by
sycophants and place-hunters ? If the shadows are
dark around him, he does but shine forth the clearer
from their midst. Fate, with the judgement of a
master-hand, drew him apart from the brilliant
ever-shifting hues, the ceaseless movement of that
dazzling, multi-coloured throng, and placed him,
alone, against that darker background of Cambrai.
The ray that illumines that pale, ascetic face, vic-
torious in defeat, is from heaven and can never fade.
Divine indeed was the hand that ' shaped that end,'
consecrating to posterity a memory at once so
fragrant, so gracious, and so pure.

It must have been about this time that Fénelon
addressed to his lifelong friend, the Abbé Langeron,
an ode descriptive of the beauties of the country
round Carennac. If it is not to be regarded as great
poetry, it is certain that its author would have been
the last to make such a claim for it. These verses are
the sort of graceful, half-playful composition which
any man of taste and culture with an eye sensitive to
natural beauty might have thrown off to beguile a
vacant hour, knowing that the friend to whom they
were addressed would accept them with an indulgent
eye as ' the perfume and suppliance of a minute,'
and love them for their writer's sake. The poem
consists of fourteen stanzas of ten lines each. The

following will give a sufficient indication of the tone
and quality of the whole :

> Montagnes de qui l'audace
> Va porter jusques aux cieux
> Un front d'éternelle glace
> Soutien du séjour des dieux ;
> Dessus vos têtes chenues
> Je cueille au-dessus des nues
> Toutes les fleurs du printemps.
> A mes pieds, contre la terre,
> J'entends gronder le tonnerre
> Et tomber mille torrents.
>
> Mais dans ce rude paysage,
> Où tout est capricieux,
> Et d'une beauté sauvage,
> Rien ne rappelle à mes yeux
> Les bords que mon fleuve arrose,
> Fleuve où jamais le vent n'ose
> Les moindres flots soulever,
> Où le ciel serein nous donne
> Le printemps après l'automne
> Sans laisser place à l'hiver.
>
> Solitude, où la rivière
> Ne laisse entendre autre bruit
> Que celui d'une onde claire
> Qui tombe, écume et s'enfuit,
> Où deux îles fortunées,
> De rameaux verts couronnées
> Font, pour le charme des yeux,
> Tout ce que le coeur désire,
> Que ne puis-je, sur ma lyre,
> Te chanter du chant des dieux !
>
> En quelque climat que j'erre,
> Plus que tous les autres lieux,
> Cet heureux coin de la terre
> Me plaît, et rit à mes yeux ;
> Là, pour couronner ma vie,
> La main d'une Parque amie
> Filera mes plus beaux jours ;
> Là reposera ma cendre ;
> Là Tyrcis viendra répandre
> Les pleurs dus à nos amours.

Not perhaps of the very purest Helicon, but musical
and pleasing, as the waters of his own smooth-
flowing Dordogne.

> Où le ciel serein nous donne
> Le printemps après l'automne
> Sans laisser place à l'hiver

recalls the lines in *The Tempest* :

> Spring come to you, at the farthest,
> In the very end of harvest,

or the words of Amos :

> ' The ploughman shall overtake the reaper.'

The first stanza, it is true, is descriptive rather of
le Périgord Noir than of Quercy, but all the rest sings
of the ' happy fields ' of Carennac.

Of a like charm in their literary allusiveness are
some lines which he wrote to Bossuet at Germigny,
the country residence of the Bishops of Meaux :

> De myrte et de laurier, de jasmins et de roses,
> De lys, de fleurs d'orange en son beau sein écloses,
> Germigny se couronne, et sème les plaisirs.

He bids the North Wind spare this pleasant abode :

> Taisez-vous, aquilons, dont l'insolente rage
> Attaque le printemps, caché dans son bocage. . . .

He calls on the mountains and forests round about to
protect their treasure against the Winter's rude
assault :

> Hiver, cruel hiver, dont frémit la nature,
> Ah ! si tu flétrissais cette vive peinture !
> Hâtez-vous donc, forêts, montagnes d'alentour,
> Défendez votre gloire, arrêtez son audace.
> Tremblez, nymphes, tremblez, c'est Tempé qu'il menace,
> Des grâces et des jeux c'est le riant séjour.

' There, my Lord,' he concludes, ' such are
the rhymes that a friend of mine sends you,

begging you to repeat them to Germigny, by way of consolation for the sufferings of the season. We received the letter that was sent from Meaux the very day you left Paris. We noted and admired its diligence. . . . I have no news, for there is nothing new in my telling you that I am—what I ought to be, but what I must not say, seeing that you forbid me any compliments in my letters.'

CHAPTER III

POLEMIST AND PREACHER

WHEN, after his ordination, Fénelon quitted the Seminary of Saint-Sulpice, he went to live with his uncle, the Marquis Antoine, to whom the King had granted quarters in the Abbaye of Saint-Germain des Prés. Saint-Simon's description of him at this period is not a flattering one. 'For a long time,' he says, 'Fénelon had knocked, and knocked in vain, at every possible door. Having applied without success to the Jesuits, as the fount from which all ecclesiastical blessings might be expected to flow, he betook himself in some pique to the Jansenists. It was a considerable time before he succeeded in insinuating himself into their good graces, but at last he contrived to get himself received into the distinguished company who were wont to dine two or three times a week under the roof of the Duchesse de Brancas. But whether it was that he seemed a little too subtle for their taste, or whether he was looking for quicker advancement than he was likely to gain with people who had nothing to share with him but their wounded feelings, his relations with them gradually cooled off. At last, however, by assiduously frequenting Saint-Sulpice, he succeeded in forming another connexion from which he expected better things.'

In brief, the young Abbé, whose only assets were his wits and his family connexions, was by no means devoid—at least so it seemed to Saint-Simon—of worldly ambitions. Be it remembered, however, that where a man's actions were susceptible of a worldly, or an unworldly interpretation, Saint-Simon could always be relied upon to choose the former. Moreover, he had not met Fénelon at this time, and had no personal knowledge of him by which to correct his impressions. And so Saint-Simon wrote him down as full of ambition, with no lack of the *savoir-faire* requisite for its realisation. Nevertheless, the day was to come when this man, reputedly so clever and so eager for advancement, was to make so light of what the world had to offer as wilfully to disdain its most coveted prizes just as they came within his grasp. And for what ? For a mere nothing, the general run of people would have answered ; for a whim, a caprice, a piece of the sheerest quixotry ! But was he so ambitious ? Was he indeed the kind of conscienceless sycophant who, having been rebuffed by one party, would, out of mere resentment, offer his services to their sworn adversaries ? De Harlay, that very worldly prelate, anxious to attract the coming men to himself and away from Bossuet, whose growing influence was beginning to alarm him, made flattering overtures to Fénelon. Fénelon coldly waved them aside, eliciting from de Harlay a response that has passed into history. ' You want to be forgotten, M. l'Abbé ? ' he said ; adding bitterly as he turned away : ' Well, then, you *shall* be ! ' Hardly ambitious that ; for de Harlay, who had great influence with the King, could undoubtedly have pushed him far. Moreover, if Fénelon had been the kind of talented schemer that Saint-Simon portrays, would he have made the friends he did ? Would he have won and retained through all the vicissitudes of his career the affection of some of the purest and loftiest spirits of the time ? The de Beauvilliers, the de Chevreuses, Mme de Luynes, Mme de Mortemart, Mme de Maintenon—they could tell false metal from true, they were not to be deceived by hypocrisy masquerading as religion, however cunning the disguise. The de Beauvilliers and the de Chevreuses became his lifelong and unswerving friends, standing by him in the hours of his darkest adversity, when others, fearful of incurring the King's displeasure, disowned him, or held warily aloof. If then he had ambition—and no doubt he had—it was an honourable ambition, an ambition that was never allowed to clash with his conscience. He was something more, as we shall shortly see, than the merely clever young man bent on improving his fortunes, that Saint-Simon saw in him at this time. For one thing, he was a genius—and genius will speak with most miraculous organ.

Ambitions then we may grant him, but without reproach, and in the loftiest of causes, aspiring indeed to shine, but always *ad majorem Dei gloriam*.

As to Fénelon's abilities, Bossuet, to whom he was now closely attached, thought well enough of them to set him to work on a highly delicate and important task, which was none other than a refutation of Malebranche's treatise on *Nature and Grace*.

Père Malebranche of the Oratory was a very remarkable man. Puny, sickly, infirm, he lived, as Lemaître puts it, ' in his head,' and spent fifty years of his life pondering incessantly on the nature of God. He loved reasoning and intellectual speculation, but he was haunted by the dread lest his theories should lead him at last into unorthodoxy, and went in perpetual terror of seeing God, the object of his meditations, merge and disappear in the Laws of Nature. He had been ordained priest in the year 1664, but he had never performed any parochial or educational duties. At one time he was librarian of his Order, and afterwards Master of Ceremonies in the Oratory Church in the rue Saint-Honoré, but from these functions he dissociated himself as

MALEBRANCHE

promptly as possible in order to devote his energies
exclusively and uninterruptedly to a life of the
austerest meditation.

Malebranche's ideas tended towards Deism, even,
perhaps, towards Pantheism. According to him,
God is the centre of a complete system and is Himself
subject to an immutable and ineluctable order.
Unlike Descartes, who held that, if He had so willed,
God might have so ordained things that the three
angles of a triangle might have been together
greater, or less, than two right angles, or that He
might have imposed upon us another moral law, or
that he might have preferred an eternal world to a
world which had its beginning in Time, Malebranche argued that reason is immutable and
' necessary.' God Himself is obliged to consult
and obey it. But God consults Himself alone. It
therefore follows that reason is not something
distinct from God. God did not command that the
eternal verities should come into existence, they
are not His creatures ; they are God Himself. The
ancients believed in a Fate or Necessity to which all
the gods, even Zeus himself, were subservient.
With Malebranche, Order is not something distinct
from, and greater than God. It *is* God.

The metaphysical system of Malebranche is too
complex to admit of being presented in a brief
summary. To abridge it would be inevitably to
deform it. If it is discarded now, there remain parts
of it that are not without their value. ' There is in
Malebranche,' says Bergson, ' a whole system of
psychology and morals which still retains its value,
even if we cannot subscribe to his metaphysics.
That is one of the distinguishing marks of French
philosophy. If it sometimes condescends to become
systematic, it does not sacrifice everything to the
spirit of system. It does not so travesty the elements
of reality as not to be able to find a use for the

building materials even though the building itself
be condemned. The house may not be habitable,
but the bricks are of good quality.'

To Malebranche's rationalistic conception of the
universe, Fénelon in his *Réfutation* opposes a mystical
conception. His mind and heart instinctively
revolt against the cold, pitiless God of Malebranche,
remote, austere, aloof ; and he portrays, instead, a
God to whom the fate of all His creatures, even the
least of them, is a matter of infinite concern. For
Fénelon, as for Hamlet : ' There is a special providence in the fall of a sparrow.' Even now he gives
evidence of that unfailing dialectical skill, of those
incomparable powers of argument and expression
which, a few years hence, in the Quietist controversy,
he was to exercise with such dazzling effect.

His refutation of Malebranche is a proof of
Fénelon's intellectual powers. For the quality of
his soul we may go to his sermons, and particularly
one which he preached for the Feast of the Epiphany
in the Church of Foreign Missions, Paris, in the
presence of the Ambassadors of Siam. He takes for
his subject the Vocation of the Gentiles and for his
text these words from the sixtieth chapter of Isaias :

Arise, shine, O Jerusalem, for thy light is come,
and the glory of the Lord is risen upon thee.

He begins by rendering thanks to God for choosing
him to praise the work that was being accomplished
by the members of that house, the House of Foreign
Missions, in spreading the light of Faith among the
peoples of the East. ' It fills my heart with joy,' he
cries, ' to be speaking of the vocation of the Gentiles
here in this House, whence men go forth to proclaim
the glad tidings to those that have heard them not.

' No sooner was Jesus born, Jesus the hope and
desire of the world, than the Magi, noble heralds
of the Gentile races, guided by the star of Bethlehem,

drew near to behold Him and to do Him homage. Then the nations arose in countless multitudes and followed in their steps. Idols were cast down and the knowledge of the true God spread abroad abundant as the waters of the sea that flows over the earth. Behold the peoples and the princes who, generation after generation, draw near to worship Him to whom the Magi came this day, so long ago, to render homage and adoration. Ye nations of the East, ye too shall come in your turn to worship and glorify His name. A light whose glory shall outshine the stars shall blaze forth before your eyes and put to rout the shadows that surround you. Arise, tarry not, make haste and come to the House of the God of Jacob ! Jerusalem rejoice and shout aloud with gladness ! Ye who were barren and brought not forth shall be barren no longer ; countless shall be your children in those far off regions of the earth, and ye shall be filled with wonder at your own fruitfulness. Lift up your eyes round about and behold ! Let your gaze drink to the full of the glory that is yours, let your hearts be filled with tenderness and admiration. The peoples in their multitude turn their gaze upon you, the isles shall draw near unto you and the strength of the nations shall be yours. Other Magi who have seen the Star of Christ shall come forth from the innermost parts of Ind to seek Him. Arise, Jerusalem, shine, for thy light is come ! . . .

' I feel my heart stirred within me ; but it is torn twixt joy and sorrow. The apostolic mission of these saintly men and the calling to Christ of these races is the triumph of religion : but, perchance, it is also the cause of a hidden retribution that hangs over our heads. Perchance we shall be cast down and these peoples shall be exalted over us even as the Gentiles were exalted over the Jews when the Church was born. Behold here is a work wrought by God to glorify His Gospel ; what if it be also to take it from us and transfer it into other hands ? . . . They love not the Lord who love not His handiwork. . . . Let us then rejoice in the Lord, my brethren, but let our rejoicing be mingled with fear and trembling. . . .

' O Spirit promised by the fountain of all Truth to such as seek Thee, let my heart throb with this one longing, that it may draw Thee unto it and be filled with Thee. Dumb be my lips rather than they should utter aught save Thy word, and let my eyes be blind to every light save the day-spring which Thou dost shed upon us from on high. O Holy Spirit, be Thou all in all to us. Grant to these, my hearers, understanding and wisdom and tenderness of heart ; and, to me, strength, and grace, and inward illumination. O Mary, pray for us ! *Ave Maria.* . . . Jesus Christ is born and lo ! the face of the world is made new again. The law of Moses, his miracles, and the wonders wrought by the prophets had availed not to stem the torrent of idolatry and to safeguard the worship of the true God. But He that cometh from on high is above all. To Jesus it is given to possess all nations for His heritage. And His they are, as ye see. Since the day when He was lifted up on the Cross, He has drawn all men to Him. In the earliest times, St. Irenaeus and Tertullian showed that the Church's sway was wider than the Empire which claimed to embrace the earth. The wild and inaccessible regions of the North, which the sun scarce illumines with his ray, have beheld the heavenly light. The burning strands of Africa have been flooded with the tide of grace. Emperors, coming at last to adore the Name they once reviled, have become the protectors of that very Church whose blood they had caused to flow. The power of the Gospel was not exhausted by these efforts. Time avails not to stay its onward course. It comes from Jesus Christ, and He is of all time.

He was yesterday, to-day He is, He will be for ever. Seventeen hundred years after His death, His Word still lives and brings forth fruit in the remotest regions of the earth. By the fulfilment of His promise, a promise so unparalleled, so boundless, Christ shows that He holds in His undying hands the hearts of all peoples and of every generation.

'Thus it is that we still show forth the True Church to our erring brethren, even as St. Augustine showed it forth to the sectaries of his day. How glorious, my brethren, and how comforting, to speak in the same words and to reveal the same marks as did that Father of the Church thirteen hundred years ago. It is the City set upon a hill that is beheld from afar by all the peoples of the earth. It is the Kingdom of Jesus Christ which embraces all nations to whom the task of proclaiming Christ's Gospel to the heathen has been entrusted. . . .'

Then, having shown the need there must be of an authority, a visible, living authority, to explain the Scriptures, ' manifestly liable to so many contradictory interpretations,' he goes on to ask how it would fare with the humble and unlearned if there were no Church to guide them. Therefore, in addition to the unbroken succession of her pastors, by whom the truth has been handed down from generation to generation, God has endowed the Church with a singular vigour and fruitfulness in order to distinguish it from those isolated sects which languish obscurely, sterile, and inert, in this or that corner of the earth. How dare they claim, these new sects, that idolatry reigned everywhere before they came with their ' reforms ' !

'Since all nations were given by the Father to the Son, can it be that Jesus Christ cast away His heritage ? What hand more mighty than His has wrested it from Him ? Hath His light been extinguished in the world ? Peradventure, my

D

brethren, you thought those words were mine.
Not so ; it is St. Augustine that spoke those words
to the Donatists, the Manichaeans of his day, or,
with but a change of name, to the Protestants of
ours. . . .'

The sermon ends with this prayer : ' O Lord, who
didst speak in Thy Scriptures saying : " Even though
a woman forget her own child, the fruit of her
womb, I will not forget thee," turn not Thy face
from us. Let the fruit of Thy Word increase in
those kingdoms to which Thou art sending it, but
forget not Thine older Churches. Remember the
See of St. Peter, the immovable foundation of Thy
promises. Remember the Church of France, Mother
of the Eastern Church, whereon Thy Grace doth
shine. Remember this Thy House and those who
are trained within it to go forth into foreign lands,
remember their tears, their prayers, their labours.
What shall I say to Thee, O Lord, of ourselves ?
Be mindful of our sorrows and of Thine own mercy.
Remember the Blood of Thy Son, which was poured
out for us, which pleads for us, in which alone we
put our trust. Take not from us, in the name of
Thy Justice, the little faith which still is ours, but
rather give it increase, purify it, and quicken it still
more, so that it may lighten our darkness, stifle our
passions, correct our judgement, to the end that,
having faithfully believed here below, we may
hereafter behold in Thy bosom the everlasting
object of our faith. *Amen.*'

The sermon should be read as a whole ; moreover
a great part of its lyrical beauty necessarily evaporates
in translation. Nevertheless, these extracts, brief,
disjointed, and imperfectly rendered though they
be, may yet suffice to reveal something of the
spiritual quality of their author. It is all very
different, as Lemaître observes, from the pattern
followed by Bossuet, Bourdaloue, Massillon, and

the great pulpiteers of the seventeenth century. Gone are the familiar ' three parts,' and the inevitable ' conclusion '; gone the massive, architectural grandeur of phrase, hewn, as it were, from the solid rock and moulded into enduring monuments of majesty and splendour. Fénelon's sermon has the spontaneity of an improvisation, it springs from the heart, it soars aloft on unwearying wings, and his words are dipped in the hues of the morning.

And how modern is the note he sounds ! The orations of Bossuet, of Bourdaloue, bear the mark of their century upon them. They ' date,' as the saying goes. But those words of Fénelon's might have been uttered yesterday. Is not this an echo of them ? ' Coming to you, then, from the very time of the Apostles, spreading out into all lands, triumphing over a thousand revolutions, exhibiting so awful a unity, glorying in so mysterious a vitality, so majestic, so imperturbable, so bold, so saintly, so sublime, so beautiful, O ye sons of men, can ye doubt that she is the Divine Messenger for whom you seek ? O long sought after, tardily found, desire of the eyes, joy of the heart, the truth after many shadows, the fullness after many foretastes, the home after many storms, come to her, poor wanderers, for she it is, and she alone, who can unfold the meaning of your being and the secret of your destiny. She alone can open to you the gate of heaven and put you on your way. "Arise, shine, O Jerusalem, for thy light is come, and the glory of the Lord is risen upon thee." ' Is not that the very note, the very cry that rings in those words of Fénelon ? Compare again this with what Fénelon says of those ' sects which languish obscurely, sterile, and inert, in this or that corner of the earth ' : ' How different . . . are all religions that ever were, from this lofty and unchangeable Catholic Church ! They depend on time and place for their

existence, they live in periods or in regions. They
are children of the soil, indigenous plants, which
readily flourish under a certain temperature, in a
certain aspect, in moist or in dry, and die if they are
transplanted. . . . Some accident gives rise to these
religious manifestations ; some sickly season, the
burning sun, the vapour-laden marsh, breeds a
pestilence, and there it remains, hanging in the air
over its birthplace perhaps for centuries ; then
some change takes place in the earth or in the
heavens, and it suddenly is no more.' Those
extracts are from a sermon preached by one whose
voice is remembered by many men yet living—
John Henry Newman.

About this time, Fénelon composed his *Dialogues
on Eloquence*, especially pulpit eloquence. They are
in the main a plea for naturalness and sincerity, and
a warning to those ' brilliant ' preachers who are
more concerned for their own reputation as orators,
than for the dissemination of Catholic truth. Most
of the conclusions arrived at in these *Dialogues*,
however, are contained in the *Letter to the Academy*,
and the *Dialogues* themselves need not be analysed
in detail. It is otherwise with a work which will be
considered in the next chapter.

CHAPTER IV

A MANUAL FOR MOTHERS

MADAME DE BEAUVILLIERS had a numerous family. The girls alone numbered eight, to say nothing of the boys. And Madame de Beauvilliers, who had come under the Fénelonian spell, begged the young Abbé to give her some ideas as to how they should be brought up. Fénelon complied, and the *Traité de l'Éducation des Filles* was the result. It filled a long-standing gap in pedagogic literature. Not, exactly, that it could be described as *proles sine matre creata*. It had had its forerunners : the *Oeconomicus* of Xenophon, for example, gives some sound advice on the training of daughters. Then there are the letters of St. Jerome to Lacta, which deal more expressly with the inward life ; and the conversations of Erasmus, which treat mainly of points of behaviour and etiquette. There is also Mlle de Scudéry ; but she, who was once acclaimed as ' the illustrious Sapho,' is readable no longer.

Madame de Beauvilliers' daughters were too young for Fénelon to give advice concerning each one separately, varying the curriculum according to their several abilities, tastes, and temperaments. He therefore had to treat his subject generally, propounding views and maxims that he thought appropriate to the sex as a whole. This exquisite little ' Manual for Mothers ' is the outcome of his excogitations. Fénelon was now in his early thirties. His vocation, his upbringing—he had been

taken away from home when he was twelve—would
have afforded him scanty opportunity for frequenting
the society of women, yet it will now be seen what a
remarkable insight he possessed into the feminine
heart and mind.

According to Macaulay, the literary stores of a
seventeenth-century lady-of-the-manor generally
consisted of a prayer-book and a book of recipes.
' If,' says Macaulay, ' a damsel had the least smatter-
ing of literature, she was regarded as a prodigy.
Ladies highly born, highly bred, and naturally
quick-witted, were unable to write a line in their
mother-tongue without solecisms and faults of
spelling such as a charity girl would now be ashamed
to commit.' In France, the standard of feminine
culture seems to have been pretty much the same.
' It would be a highly startling thing,' said the Abbé
Fleury, ' to maintain that women should be taught
anything but the catechism, needlework, singing,
dancing, how to curtsey gracefully and speak
correctly ; for that, as a rule, is all their education
amounts to.' On the other hand, it must be admitted
that, in 1672 or thereabouts, a Protestant writer,
one Poulain de la Barre, a pupil of Descartes, in
his treatise, *The Equality of the Sexes*, had advanced
some theories which would have taken the wind
out of the sails of the most advanced ' feminists '
of these days. ' If,' he says, ' we should think it
comic to see women playing the part of policemen,
barristers, judges, generals, pastors, or ambassadors,
that is only because we are not used to it. The
novelty would soon wear off.' It is two hundred and
fifty years since Poulain de la Barre wrote that.
Women-barristers, women-professors we have long
been used to ; even the policewoman no longer
excites a smile. He would be a bold man who
should assert that the army and the *Corps-diplo-
matique* will for ever remain closed to women.

Fénelon stopped a good deal short of this, yet he advocated some innovations that were startling enough in their day. ' Fénelon's treatise,' according to Janet, ' marks the beginning of all later developments in female education.' The work was of course at first a purely private affair, but the young Abbé's observations and advice seemed so richly fraught with insight and common sense, that he was urged to put it into print. It was owing to these pressing representations that in 1687 he gave it, the first of his published works, to the world.

The opening words strike the keynote of the whole. They are clear and sharp. He does not argue ; he asserts. ' Nothing is more neglected than girls' education.' ' Look,' he says, ' at the boys on the other hand. For them no trouble, no expense is spared. Look at the money spent on their books and the instruments for scientific research ; look at the trouble that is taken to teach them foreign languages, and so forth. As for girls, they are taught nothing, lest they might be taught too much. It is currently held that an interest in things intellectual makes them vain and affected. It is quite enough for them to learn to manage a house and obey their husbands. The supporters of this theory are not slow in quoting examples to show what a ridiculous creature book-learning will make of a woman.' Arguments like this were, according to Fénelon, usually regarded as sufficient justification for handing over girl-children to the care of a mother who was very possibly as ignorant as she was thoughtless. ' No one,' he freely admits, ' wants to make that absurd thing, a blue-stocking, of any girl; but in learning, as in everything else, there is the golden mean. Women, as a rule, have less intellectual stamina and more inquisitiveness than men. Therefore, it would be inappropriate to set them to study too deeply and perhaps make prigs of them for your

trouble. They don't have to rule the country, go
to the wars, or become priests. This being so, there
is no need for them to embark upon such extensive
fields of study as are required by politics, the art of
war, jurisprudence, philosophy, and theology. The
majority of the mechanical arts are unsuited to them,
unsuited to their physique. Girls are made for
moderate exercises. Neither their bodies nor their
minds are so strong, so robust as a man's. On the
other hand, Nature has made them industrious, and
endowed them with a taste for orderliness and
household management, so as to keep them quietly
and comfortably at home.'

' But,' asks Fénelon, ' if women are naturally the
weaker vessels, what then ? The weaker they are, the
more important it is to strengthen them. Have they
not duties to fulfil, duties which are at the basis of
all human life ? Is it not they who make or mar
the happiness of their households, who regulate
every detail of family life and who, therefore, have
control of everything which most intimately concerns
the human race ? From which it follows that they
are the determining factor in the good or evil
behaviour of well-nigh the whole world. A woman
of poise and judgement, who punctually attends to
her duties, domestic and religious, is the guiding
spirit of the whole house. She so orders it as to
provide for the welfare, spiritual and temporal, of
all its inmates. Nay, man, who in public affairs
has unfettered authority, can give no real effect to
his resolutions unless woman lends him her co-operation. The world is not an abstraction, a figment of
the imagination ; it is the aggregate of all the
families composing it. Who then is in a better
position to supervise it than woman, than the
mistress of the house, who, besides her position of
authority and her continual presence in the house,
is by nature careful, attentive to detail, industrious,

engaging, and persuasive ? What sweetness or charm may a man look for in life if its most intimate relationship, namely marriage, is turned to bitterness and gall ? And the children, that is to say the world of to-morrow, how will they grow up, if their mother spoils them from their tenderest years ?

' A woman's occupations are hardly less important to the common weal than a man's. She has a home to manage, a husband to bless, and children to educate. Virtue is as essential in a woman as in a man—men think more so—and apart from the good or evil they can do in the world, they form one half of the human race redeemed by the blood of Jesus Christ and destined to eternal life.'

Then Fénelon invites us to consider not only the good which woman does when she is well brought up, but the evil she brings to pass in the world when she lacks the virtues that a good training inspires. It cannot be doubted that defective female education is more productive of harm in the world than defective male education, since the sins of men often arise from the ill-training they had from their mother, or from the passions with which, when they came to manhood, other women inspired them. ' What tales of intrigue,' exclaims Fénelon, ' does not History bring before us, what subversions of law and morality, what sanguinary wars, what onslaughts on religion, what revolutions in the state—and all caused by the lawlessness of woman ! ' (This is manifestly an allusion to the Fronde and to the women who played so conspicuous a part in that curtain-raiser to the Great Revolution.)

Having thus made it clear how all-important it is that women should be educated, he proceeds to inquire *how* they should be educated. ' Let us see,' he says, ' in what that education should consist.'

According to Fénelon, education can hardly begin too soon. The passions are present and active even

in infancy, and it is touch and go how they will
turn out. Had not St. Augustine seen an infant,
its face pale with fury, glaring with every mark of
hatred at its hungry rival at the breast ? 'The
child,' says Fénelon, 'just beginning to babble its
mother-tongue will soon learn to employ it with an
ease and a mastery that will throw the achievements
of the adult student laboriously acquiring a dead
language completely into the shade.' 'The brain
of a child,' he goes on, ' is moist and tender and,
therefore, the impressions it receives are deep as
well as lasting, far deeper and far more lasting than
when it has been dried and hardened by the process
of the years. The fact that the child-mind is
susceptible of these enduring impressions, these
vivid and ineffaceable images, explains why elderly
people recall the scenes and events of their earlier
years more clearly than those of recent occurrence.'
' How often,' he says, ' is the power of those early
impressions to mould our lives for good or ill
unconsciously admitted by people who say : " No ;
this is my line, my bent. This is how I was brought
up to look at the matter. I cannot change now."
In proportion then, as these early impressions are
deep and potent, it behoves us to see that they
are salutary and not baneful.'

But though young children are quick to receive
impressions, the power to reflect and to reason upon
them is only gained by discipline and patience.
Fénelon likens the mental processes of a child to a
candle burning in a draught. The flame is never
steady. 'A child asks you a question and before
you have time to answer he is wool-gathering, gazing
up at the ceiling counting the rafters, or at the
window wondering how many panes of glass there
are in it. And when you endeavour to recall him
to the matter in hand, he shows signs of impatience
and constraint, like one chafing at his prison bars.

Therefore we should beware of imposing heavy
burdens upon his faculties while yet they are but
nascent and unable to bear them. Answer what he
asks you freely; let him ply you with questions to
the top of his bent; encourage and sustain his
curiosity; enrich his memory with a fund of good
material.' Thus Fénelon; and in all this he is
borne out by another great writer, he too a Catholic
and an ecclesiastic, to whom, not only in his definite
views and opinions, but still more in the general
tone and temper of his mind, he bears so close a
resemblance. Nearly two hundred years after the
publication of Fénelon's treatise, Newman in that
magnificent ' tractate on education ' which he called
The Idea of a University, wrote as follows : ' A boy's
business when he goes to school is to learn, that is,
to store up things in his memory. For some years
his intellect is little more than an instrument for
taking in facts, or a receptacle for storing them ; he
welcomes them as fast as they come to him ; he lives
on what is without; he has his eyes ever about
him ; he has a lively susceptibility of impressions ;
he imbibes information of every kind ; and little
does he make his own in a true sense of the word,
living rather upon his neighbours all around him.
. . . It is the seven years of plenty with him ; he
gathers in by handfuls, like the Egyptians, without
counting.' But Newman's concern in the volume
from which that extract is taken, is with a later
stage in the educational process, namely the philo-
sophising of knowledge, the systematisation of the
multifarious facts acquired, with the recognition of
relationships between them, and of their inter-
dependence one upon another ; in short, with the
transformation of the man of facts, the ' know-
ledgeable ' man, the ' well-informed ' man, into the
man of ideas, the philosopher. In other words, it
is not enough ' to read, mark, learn ' ; we must also

' inwardly digest.' Our knowledge is not really ours
till it has become part of our very tissue, till it has
entered into our blood and bone.

On one thing Fénelon lays particular stress and
that is that ' lessons ' should never be allowed to
assume a harsh or forbidding aspect, never be
associated in the mind of the learner with ' constraint, boredom, or severity.' Just as he condemns
the practice of scaring children into obedience with
talk of black-robed priests and hideous ghosts that
walk by night, so he emphasises the necessity of
making lessons pleasurable and attractive, and of
reducing constraint and punishment to the minimum.
' Don't bore and depress children,' he says, ' by
perpetually talking to them in schoolmaster's jargon
about things they can't understand. Don't let
" school " or " class " spell no freedom, no liveliness,
everlasting lessons, silence, constrained postures,
grumbling, and perpetual threats. On the other
hand, if you *do* threaten, carry out your threat, but
only as a last resort ; because, if you do not, your
power to maintain discipline will be at an end.' So
important does it seem to Fénelon to make the
acquisition of knowledge agreeable, that he regards
it as a serious disqualification in a tutor to exhibit
any physical abnormalities calculated to repel or
disgust his pupil. ' People,' he says, ' may be
patterns of propriety, models of piety and yet
anything but good to look upon. It is a mistake to
try to force children to take to them.'

In all this, there is a good deal which foreshadows
that method of education which is known as the
Dalton Plan, without the exaggerations by which
that plan is occasionally rendered ridiculous.

But, to say the truth, Fénelon fought shy of plans.
In contrast to Sir Austin Feverel, he had a profound
distrust of educational systems. He believed that
the sort of education a child received should depend

on the character and temperament of that particular
child, considered in connexion with the position
which he, or she, would be called upon to fill in
after life. With the Duc de Bourgogne, Fénelon
did not forget that he was one day to be king ;
with Mademoiselle de Beauvilliers, that, in due
course, she would be the mistress of a house.

'A woman has a social duty to perform whose
importance it is impossible to exaggerate. See to
it, then, that her education is such as to enable her
to perform it with credit.'

'From the moral point of view, too, an occupied
mind is necessary to banish dangerous longings, to
counteract morbid sensibility, to withstand the
wave of passion to which too many women succumb.
A sound moral and intellectual training forearms a
woman against the baneful effects of reading sensational novels and the bitter disillusionment which is
commonly its sequel. A poor girl with her head
full of the tender and wonderful things she has
read about in books is dismayed to find that they
have no counterpart in real life. She would like
to live like the heroines of these romances, always
charming, always adorable, whose slightest whims
are always gratified. What a grim awakening, to
come down from heights like those to the humdrum
details of everyday domestic existence.' In Fénelon's
age, as in every other, there was no lack of Emma
Bovarys.

The mistress of a big country-house—the Squire's
lady, let us say—ought to know a good deal about
domestic economy and even estate management.
She must, therefore, be thoroughly conversant with
the three ' R's ' ; a little knowledge of the Law and
of History should also be hers, and, by way of
accomplishments, an acquaintance with the best
standard writers in prose and poetry. There would
be no use in her wasting her time over Italian and

Spanish ; a little Latin would be far more profitable.
Painting and music ? Perhaps; but in cautious doses.
The chief thing for a woman—next, of course, to
her religious duties—is to know how to manage a
house, and that is no easy matter if it is to be done
with skill and judgement. No doubt a woman
should be economical, thrifty ; but she must not
be fussy over trifles. She should beware of becoming
the penny-wise and pound-foolish sort of person
who makes a great to-do about economising on the
candles, and allows some crafty and unprincipled
steward to cheat her out of pounds.

' If a woman would gain the respect and obedience
of her servants, she herself must have a practical
knowledge of the details of cooking and housework.
It is no good chiding the cook for taking too long to
make an omelet, if you yourself don't know how long
it should take ; no good blaming her for putting too
much sugar in the pudding, if you haven't got the
recipe at your fingers' ends.'

The *maîtresse de maison* he has in mind in all his
descriptions is one whom he had had some opportunity of studying. If Fénelon's mother was a great
lady, gracious and cultivated, she was also, and by
necessity, as thrifty and saving as any Scottish
housewife. Not, indeed, grimly, selfishly, stingily
saving—far from it ; but generously, warm-
heartedly, cheerfully studying ways and means for
the comfort and well-being of all about her—
husband, sons, daughters, down to the lowliest of
her dependants, and to the poor about her gates.

If the portrait with which Fénelon concludes his
treatise is that of the virtuous woman of the Bible,
it is also that of her whom we may call the Laird's
wife, or her Périgourdin counterpart ; of the lady of
the house, manor, *gentilhommière*, or castle, who sees
that all runs punctually and smoothly, and keeps the
servants at their work, what time her lord is com-

bining business with pleasure, perhaps in Paris, perhaps no further than the neighbouring market-town. Périgord, the ancient home of his race, the memories of his frugal and happy childhood, were in his mind clearly enough when he recommended that great Court lady, the Duchesse de Beauvilliers, to teach her daughters to be ' careful of the gear.' If Fénelon adumbrates a curriculum that seems more appropriate to the wife of a needy country squire who will have all her work cut out to make the two ends meet and to present a respectable front to the world, than to a lady destined to play a conspicuous part at the most brilliant of all royal Courts, we may take it that the scenes and circumstances of his childhood were still present to his mind, the memories of that beloved old home—half-fortress, half-farm—by the Dordogne, with its familiar, spacious, but scantily-furnished rooms, its tarnished splendours so eloquent of noble poverty, where long ago he had learned, and never afterwards forgot,

Angustam amice pauperiem pati.

So, too, of his methods with the Duc de Bourgogne. How often he seems to be addressing himself to a country squire, or gentleman-farmer, rather than to the heir of the most splendid throne in Europe.

But Fénelon's treatise was primarily concerned with the education of girls. He saw how difficult and delicate a task it is to preserve the golden mean between frivolity, empty-headedness on the one hand, and priggishness and pedantry on the other.

The *Mercure* of 1752 contains the panegyric of a certain Madame de Labrousse, Comtesse de Verteillac, from which we can trace the lineaments of a woman such as Fénelon would assuredly have commended : ' Madame de Verteillac had many accomplishments, but never paraded them. She

wrote books of charm and solid merit, yet, with a
modesty almost unknown in the annals of female
authorship, she did her utmost to conceal their
origin. She could talk with ease and confidence to
learned men, and listen to their discourse with
understanding. Yet, notwithstanding all these intellectual interests, she did not disdain—far from it—
those lighter feminine graces which are indispensable
to the smooth running of the social machine.' If
Madame de Verteillac may be regarded as a product
of the sort of feminine education to which Fénelon
gave his blessing, then Fénelon had no small cause
for satisfaction. What a contrast she affords to some
of the great ladies of the age, to the odious, conceited,
and entirely unbearable little Duchesse du Maine,
for example, the incarnation of pedantry and priggish
pretentiousness who, nevertheless, gathered about
her at Sceaux so many brilliant luminaries in the
intellectual firmament of the times.

CHAPTER V

THE MISSIONER

FÉNELON'S success at the *Nouvelles Catholiques*, where his persuasiveness and charm had wrought marvels, led the authorities to employ his gifts and abilities on another part of the missionary field ; they sent him to Saintonge and Aunis to supplement the proselytising efforts— likely, as it seemed, to prove more dazzling than durable—of the soldiers who had been sent there to 'persuade' the recalcitrant Huguenots at the point of the bayonet.

Much has been written of Fénelon's *tolérantisme*, of the spirit of toleration he has been said to have displayed in this new task to which he was now called to apply himself. Now, if tolerance be synonymous with *laisser-faire*, if its significance be conveyed in such a phrase as ' live and let live,' or ' everyone has a right to his own opinion,' then tolerant he certainly was not, though his *tolérantisme* is a quality for which he has been both praised and blamed ; blamed by the zealots of his own and later times, praised and claimed as one of themselves by the philosophers of the succeeding generation. Some epigrammatist has described tolerance as the virtue of sceptical ages. Many men are praised for being tolerant when, in truth, they are but indifferent. Fénelon had a burning and unquenchable faith in the divine mission of the Catholic Church. How then should he have failed to do everything in his power to bring into its fold all those who were outside it ? The object, the goal was plain. The

only question was how best to attain it. *Force
majeure*, coercive or violent measures, threats or
intimidation—in these he, who was later on to prove
himself so skilled and delicate a director of con-
sciences, put no faith at all. But we must make no
mistake. He rejected these means, not because they
were harsh, but because they were ineffectual. We
may search in vain in his correspondence or in any
other of his writings for the smallest hint that he
condemned the revocation of the Edict of Nantes.
He not only approved of the measures taken to prevent the Huguenots leaving the country, he called
for their extension, demanding that a stricter watch
should be kept between Bordeaux and the coast.
Some of the newly converted officers, he complained,
were slack in the performance of their duties ; others,
he affirmed, connived at, or actively assisted, the
escape of their erstwhile co-religionists. Such men,
he said, should be shipped off to Canada, where
they could do no mischief.

And yet gentleness and persuasion, though not
native to the region of his origin—*brusquerie*, rather
than *douceur* is the characteristic of the people there
—are seen in perfection in this Périgourdin. ' It
were an easy matter,' said he, speaking of these
Huguenots, ' to bring them in droves to confession
and communion, if all we wanted to do was to adver-
tise our missions. But what a sham, to compel
people to come to confession when they have no
belief in the Church, or in her power to grant the
remission of sins ! How should we give Jesus
Christ to those who believe not that they are receiving
Him ? However, I do know that, where the mission-
aries and the military combine their efforts, the new
converts come flocking to communion. These
dour and stubborn folk, whose minds are so poisoned
against our religion, are yet selfish and craven. Press
them, force them never so little, and they will

commit sacrilege over and over again. For ourselves, we should fear to draw the most frightful curse upon our head if we contented ourselves with doing some hasty and superficial work that would look dazzling at a distance.' After all, if their leader had thought Paris worth a Mass, there was nothing to marvel at in the rank and file purchasing peace and quiet on the same terms.

The Government's aim was to make as many converts as possible in the shortest possible time. Quantity, not quality, was the order of the day. 'There are no more Huguenots!'—that was what they wanted to announce to the King, caring not a jot whether or not they turned these Huguenots into atheists.

If the King had waxed pious, and was anxious to strike a resounding blow for the Church by stamping out Protestantism once and for all, it was on the secular arm that he chiefly relied. It was numbers that counted with the King. If souls were important, heads were still more so.

Much has been made of the difference in the treatment meted out by the authorities—both ecclesiastical and civil—towards the Protestants on the one hand, and to the sceptics and unbelievers on the other. While the former were the victims of stern and unrelenting repression, the atheists got off scot-free. Go to a Protestant conventicle and it went hard with you; go nowhere at all, you were left alone and nothing said. A most unchristian injustice, some will exclaim, not without some *prima facie* justification. What better evidence, they will ask, could you have of the persecuting temper of the Roman Catholics? Yet such differentiation, in the circumstances, was neither so illogical nor so unjust. It was not illogical for this reason : an atheist is not a sectarian. He declines the mysteries of your religion, but he sets up no rival in its place. He may almost be regarded as a Catholic in abeyance. From the point of view of the State his fault is negative, not positive, passive not active. There is something wanting in him, and it would be as uncharitable to punish him for that short-coming as it would be to penalise him for being colour-blind, or hard-of-hearing. But, on your own authority, to set up a new religion, a rival religion, what was this but wilfully to rend the garment? What was this but schism? And schism of a peculiarly pernicious type, since it was soon seen to be capable of producing other schisms almost infinite in number and variety. In England this schism made its appearance in a singularly insidious manner. For some time after the unifying principle, allegiance to the Pope, was discarded, the outward forms of worship were suffered to remain unchanged. When he broke with the Papacy, it was neither the policy nor the desire of Henry VIII to tamper with the externals of public worship. On the contrary, this ' Defender of the Faith ' showed himself very anxious to retain them. He would have had the Mass go on just as it always had, with no change in doctrine or in ceremonial. But the Church in England—soon to become the Church *of* England—was as a branch severed from the trunk. It continued to flourish and to put forth leaves—for a time. But at length the sap was exhausted, the leaves withered and, if the branch remained, it was as something from which all supernatural life had departed. It was no longer a part of a mystical whole, drawing its sustenance from the True Vine ; it was, and is, notwithstanding all the efforts that have been made to invest it with the stately splendours of Catholic ceremonial, a politico-legal institution, a department of State, exercising no jurisdiction, wielding no authority, enjoying no prestige beyond Britain and her dominions, and there only in a very limited degree.

The Huguenots, then, were the declared and
active enemies of a religion which the atheists, or as
we should call them in these days, the agnostics,
merely disregarded. Therefore the agnostics were
disregarded in their turn, provided they did not
conspicuously parade their unbelief. A Catholic
would necessarily deplore their lack of faith. He
would never cease to hope and pray for them, but
he would not invoke the civil power against them.

But the religious and spiritual side of the matter
was not the only one. There was the political
aspect. The religious bond is a very strong one,
stronger sometimes than the bond of race. What,
asked Louis, if religious disaffection should lead to
political disaffection and so to the treasonable
commerce of the malcontents with the enemies of
their country ? These, then, are the reasons why the
Protestants were treated with severity, when atheists,
provided they made no attempt to propagate their
atheism, were usually unmolested.

Owing to the way in which the facts have been
selected and coloured for British, that is to say, for
Protestant consumption, it is generally the case that
the Huguenots are looked upon in this country as
meek and long-suffering martyrs, suffering the
cruellest persecution at the hands of their bigoted
and ruthless Catholic adversaries. All the lambs are
Protestant, all the wolves, Catholic. Such is the
effect of that cunning manipulation, or rather
selection, of evidence which goes by the name of
propaganda. Its two main weapons are *suppressio
veri* and *suggestio falsi*. If the latter is employed with
comparative restraint by the enemies of Catholicism,
they observe no such economy in their use of
suppressio veri. English schoolboys, for example,
hear a great deal about the enormities perpetrated
by the Catholics against the Protestants in the reign
of Queen Mary (whom they never neglect to call

'Bloody' Mary), they are told little or nothing—
generally nothing—about the cruelties commanded,
or connived at, by Queen Elizabeth, or 'Good
Queen Bess,' against the Catholics.

It was a serious shock to discover that Cranmer,
whom one had learnt to look upon as a hero and a
martyr, was, in fact, a poltroon and a timeserver who
combined a most unheroic elasticity of conscience
with a remarkable literary gift. It came as a still
more startling revelation to read of the tortures
inflicted on Catholics, the hangings, the drawings
and quarterings, that are described by Newman on
pages 215–218 of his *Present Position of Catholics in
England*. For example : ' Thomas Sherwood, after
six months' imprisonment in a dark and filthy hole,
was hanged, cut down alive, dismembered, bowelled,
and quartered. Alexander Brian had needles thrust
under his nails, was torn upon the rack, hanged and
beheaded. George Haydock was suffered to hang
but a very little while, when the Sheriff ordered the
rope to be cut and the whole butchery to be performed on him while he was alive and perfectly
sensible '; and so on. ' What,' asks Newman, ' will
the Protestants bring against the Holy See compar-
able to atrocities such as these ? Not surely, with
any fairness the burnings in Queen Mary's reign,
the acts, as they were of an English party, inflamed
with rage against their enemies, and opposed by
Cardinal Pole, the Pope's Legate, as well as by the
ecclesiastics of Spain.' ' These horrors,' he continues, ' are no anomaly in the history of Protestantism. . . . It has persecuted in England, in Scotland,
in Ireland, in Holland, in France, in Germany, in
Geneva ; Calvin burnt a Socinian, Cranmer an
Anabaptist, Luther advised the wholesale murder of
the fanatical peasants, and Knox was a party to
bloody enactments and bloody deeds.' ' What,'
asks Lemaître, in his turn, ' of all the Protestant

" St. Bartholomews " which, particularly in the South, preceded or followed the Catholic St. Bartholomew ? '

To return. Fénelon's tolerance was not of the breed that is synonymous with indifference. But he was a disbeliever in the efficacy of violence and constraint. The truth conveyed in the familiar adage : ' A man convinced against his will is of the same opinion still ' was always present to his mind. He would rather have made one genuine convert, than have brow-beaten a thousand into craven, hypocritical submission.

CHAPTER VI

THE ROYAL PRECEPTOR

ON August 17, 1689 Fénelon was made tutor to the Duc de Bourgogne. Everywhere the news of his appointment was received with enthusiasm. Fénelon's merits had long been recognised. In the places where he had laboured as a missionary he had left a kind of fragrance behind him and the people there remembered not only his great intellectual gifts, but those rarer attributes of gentleness, patience, and persuasiveness, that power of entering into the minds of others and seeing things through their eyes, which did more to disarm hostility and opposition than any arguments however cogent, however brilliant. It had been like the coming of the south wind after a prolonged spell of frost and snow. ' The winter is past, the rain is over and gone and the flowers have appeared again in our land.' ' This then is a Catholic priest ! ' exclaimed the astonished people, whom the King's dragoons had tried to convert by a very different method. Still, notwithstanding the reputation he enjoyed among his friends and among a certain select circle at Court, he had been living for nearly two years in a kind of penumbra, a state of semi-retirement, and none knew how, if at all, his signal gifts would be brought into requisition. But now this brilliant appointment had changed all. He had ' come out of his shell,' as Newman said when he received his Oriel fellowship. It gave him a name, a standing, in the public eye ; he became at a bound one of the notabilities of the kingdom and one of its principal adornments. Saint-Simon has drawn of him a memorable portrait : ' A tall, spare man of good figure, pale, with a prominent nose, eyes from which fire and intellectual power seemed to pour like a torrent, and a countenance the like of which I have never seen in any other man, and which, once seen, you could never forget. Everything was there in perfect combination, and the simultaneous presence of the most contradictory elements produced no effect of incongruity. In him were blended seriousness and gaiety, gravity and courtesy. He was at once the scholar, the prelate, and the *grand seigneur*. His outstanding characteristics, which seemed to impress themselves even on his material surroundings, were refinement, great intellectual gifts, wit, eloquence, decorum, and above all *noblesse*. It was difficult to take one's eyes off him. All his portraits are life-like, yet none of them have quite caught the exquisite harmony which impressed me so greatly in the original, or the exceeding delicacy of his every feature. His manner was in perfect keeping with his appearance. His ease was infectious to all around him. His conversation was marked by that charm and good taste which only come of long familiarity with the best society and the habits of the great. He possessed a natural gift of eloquence, graceful and finished, and a most insinuating yet noble and befitting courtesy ; an easy, clear, agreeable mode of speech, a marvellous gift of lucid exposition. Add to all this, that he never tried to appear cleverer than those with whom he was conversing, but always put himself on a level with them, making them feel quite at their ease.'

Such was the man on whom fortune now seemed to have made up her mind to smile with no uncertain radiance. As soon as he heard the news, Bossuet sent off a congratulatory letter to the Marquise de Laval, Fénelon's first cousin. ' Yesterday,' he says, ' my thoughts were all on the good fortune of Church and State ; but now that I've had time to realise how great must be your joy, the joy I feel myself is no less keen. I could not help thinking of that worthy and most kindly of my friends, your father, and of what his feelings would have been to-day at this blossoming forth of merits that have been at such pains to keep themselves in the background. Ah, well, Madame, we are not going to lose the Abbé Fénelon ; you will be able to enjoy his society, and I, provincial though I am, shall escape from time to time to go and embrace him.'

Among the letters of congratulation which were showered upon the new royal tutor, one stood apart. It was from the Abbé Tronson. ' You will be surprised,' it began, ' that I have not been found before this amongst the multitude of your well-wishers. I humbly beg that you will not be too hard on me for my brief delay. I felt that on an occasion which affected me so deeply, I could not do better than begin by offering my thanks to God for His dealings with you and by asking Him to bless and guide you. Both of these things I have endeavoured to the best of my ability to do, and I can now assure you how unfeignedly pleased I was to hear of your appointment. . . . But I candidly confess that my joy is not unmingled with apprehension when I think of the dangers to which you are exposed. For it cannot be denied that, in the ordinary course of things, promotion makes the way of salvation harder. It opens the door to the prizes of this world ; take heed lest it close it against the lasting guerdon of the world to come.'

After describing some of the perils and temptations that will inevitably beset him in his new and brilliant surroundings, Tronson continues : ' If ever you needed study and meditation on the Scriptures, you need them now. Hitherto you have looked to them to fortify you with the truth and to inspire you with good thoughts. Now you will need them to banish evil thoughts, and to preserve you from wickedness and falsehood. Now is the time for you to ponder well the words of St. Augustine : *Continuis vigiliis excubare, ne opinio verisimilis fallat ; ne decipiat sermo versutus.* . . . Above all, think constantly of the hour of death, when the glory of this world shall vanish like a dream, when every earthly stay shall fail you.' And then there follows a passage which shows how delicate a psychologist was this old man, almost an invalid, as he looked out upon the world from his lonely little room at Saint-Sulpice—how delicate a psychologist and how accurately he read the mind and heart of his pupil. ' No doubt,' he says, ' your friends will comfort you by telling you that you did not seek the post, and indeed, that is a definite satisfaction and a thing to thank God for. But beware of relying too much upon it. A man often has more to do with his own advancement than he imagines. It is seldom that a man really and sincerely avoids promotion. It does not follow that we always strive eagerly to win promotion ; but we are sometimes very clever in removing the obstacles that hinder our progress towards it. We may not go out of our way to curry favour with the great ; but we are rarely averse to letting them see the best side of us. It is just to these little bits of self-revelation that a man often owes his advancement, so that one can never be quite sure that one has played no part in it. . . . I am afraid you will think this a terribly long-winded epistle, more like an ill-timed sermon than a letter of congratulation. I should have made it briefer and less outspoken if I had not had your welfare so much at heart. If, in places, I have expressed myself

a little too freely, you must put it down to the love
I bear you and to my profound solicitude for your
welfare. After all the elaborate compliments you
have doubtless received from others, a little plain-
speaking from me will not come amiss.'

Nevertheless, if the fates have endowed a man with
the power and the desire to charm, it can scarcely
be imputed to him as a fault if this charm sometimes
operates to his advantage. We do not say that
Fénelon had no ambition. Quite possibly, especially
in his younger days, he had a distinct trace of worldly
aspiration and of worldly astuteness. He liked to
feel his power over men ; and he liked to put it to
the proof. That is quite possible. The time was
to come at length when he would have severed every
earthly tie, when every mundane care would have
been winnowed from his soul by ceaseless tribulation. But as a young man he may have wished, not
only to use his talents, but to win for them the
meed of public admiration. But even then there
was within his heart a refuge, a place apart, a
sanctuary into which the world and its manifold
preoccupations could never enter, a Holy of Holies
whose peace no sound of earthly turmoil could avail
to mar. The Presence that he never failed to discover
there guided him in the days of his prosperity, and
when sorrow and desolation fell upon his path, it
did not desert him.

This little Duc de Bourgogne was a child calculated to put his preceptor's pedagogic powers,
particularly his tact and his patience, to a supreme
test. Sainte-Beuve says that Fénelon must have
been greatly perturbed when he saw the material
he had got to work upon. Unless he proceeded
with great circumspection there was every probability that he would produce a Nero or a Domitian
rather than a Titus. With his violent temper, his

impetuous, unbalanced nature, his sharpness, his
undoubted cleverness, the boy had in him the
makings of something like a monster. It would be
no easy task to mould a king out of such alarming
ingredients. When the clocks struck and summoned
him to some irksome duty, this amiable scion of
royalty would promptly smash them. When rain
interfered with some out-of-door pastime or expedi-
tion on which he had set his heart, he would stamp
his feet with rage. To thwart his slightest wishes
was to send him into a paroxysm of fury. On the
other hand, there was no denying that he was clever
and quick-witted and gifted with a sharp and bitter
tongue. Nevertheless, when his storms of passion
were over he was quick to repent and confess his
fault. But he had some unpleasant traits which
urgently called for correction. For example, he
looked on the rest of mankind as inferior beings ;
even his own brothers he regarded as a sort of
intermediate breed between himself and the masses.
Truly he presented a difficult problem. Fénelon
did wisely. He discarded all theories and systems
of education, his own included, and ' made ready
for the mischance of the hour.' As Cardinal de
Bausset has it, ' he followed only one system, and
that was to have none.'

One of his expedients was, as it were, to hold the
mirror up to nature, to show virtue her own feature,
scorn her own image, by writing fables, inventing
stories, dialogues, and so forth, in which the child
might recognise himself and apply the necessary
moral. The child, it seems, had a precocious
literary talent, and these tendentious productions—
one of them, by the way, *Le Rossignol et la Fauvette*,
Sainte-Beuve considers the most exquisite of
Fénelon's writings—seemed to have had a strangely
mollifying effect. For example, the Preceptor wrote
a letter to himself purporting to come from Bayle,

the historian. It was about a medal that had recently
been discovered. Fénelon did not fail to read this
letter aloud in his pupil's hearing. ' One side of the
medal '—so the missive ran—' depicts a child of
noble bearing. Pallas holds her shield above him ;
the Graces strew his path with flowers ; Apollo,
with the nine Muses in his train, proffers him his
lyre ; Venus gliding overhead in her car lets fall
her girdle upon him ; Victory, with one hand points
to a triumphal car, and with the other, offers him a
crown. There is an inscription, taken from Horace,
reading *Non sine Dis animosus infans*.' Very charming no doubt, but now turn over. ' The reverse,'
says the imaginary letter, ' presents a very different
picture. The child is the same, but now he is
surrounded by hideous, leering faces, poisonous
snakes, blood-curdling creeping things, insects,
owls, and filthy harpies. A troop of satyrs mopping
and mowing are throwing themselves into the most
absurd contortions and pointing jeeringly at the
fish's tail which now completes the body of the
lovely child.' There is another inscription also
from Horace, *Turpiter atrum desinat in piscem.*
' Our archaeologists, numismatists, and antiquaries,'
the letter proceeds, ' are in a great quandary, being
sorely puzzled to discover on what occasion this
medal was struck. Some incline to the view that
it represents Caligula, the son of Germanicus, from
whom so much was hoped for, but who turned out a
monster. Others will have it that the boy is Nero,
who began so well and ended so disastrously.' He
would be a dull pupil who should fail to see the
application of that ; and this pupil was anything
but dull.

The Prince was fond of fables, and Fénelon freely
pandered to his taste. These fables, which Fénelon
composed, of course had morals, and the morals
were not ambiguous. For example, the boy Bacchus

DUC DE BOURGOGNE

is being taught by Silenus beneath a sacred oak, what time an impudent young Faun sits by and listens. Bacchus makes mistakes and the Faun laughs. ' What do you mean by laughing at the son of Jupiter ? ' asks the boy angrily. ' What does the son of Jupiter mean by making mistakes ? ' retorts the Faun.

Fénelon was not the only one to write fables for the Prince. La Fontaine and the boy used to have fable-writing competitions among themselves, and La Fontaine, who was also the judge, invariably lost.

But the great work of education was neither the *Fables* nor the *Dialogues of the Dead*. It was a work which attained a world-wide reputation, forming for generations, not only in France but in almost every European country, an indispensable part of the pedagogue's armoury. That work was *Télémaque*. But it is no belittlement of the virtues of that once famous book, or of the *Fables*, or of the *Dialogues*, to say that it was not they that chiefly contributed to tame and subdue this very refractory pupil. It was the steely resolution, the unconquerable will which, rather unexpectedly to those who only knew him superficially, was one of the constituents in the character of this fascinating and enigmatic preceptor. The latter did his work thoroughly. ' I know who I am and I know who you are,' said the child in a moment of hot rebellion. Before many hours were over he knew still better. Fénelon had many such encounters and won them all, sometimes by patience and persuasion, more rarely by short, sharp reprimand. But he won. He knew that to lose a single skirmish would be to lose the campaign. Authority once lost can never be recovered. He did his work thoroughly. The day came when it seemed to him that he had done it almost too thoroughly. And yet the marvel of it is that he whose will was not only tamed but broken—so, at least, most people thought—conceived no dread, no hatred of the man who had thus subdued him.   On the contrary, he never ceased to love him, even to worship him, with something like passionate devotion.

CHAPTER VII

TÉLÉMAQUE

IN the days of Fénelon—'ere yet knowledge for the million came out neatly bound in boards,' complete with introduction and notes—educational text-books were non-existent. Any tutor who had the ability, and who took his duties seriously, wrote his own text-books. Bossuet, who was tutor to the Grand Dauphin, produced for the edification of that rather 'unforthcoming' personage, the *Discours sur l'Histoire universelle*, and Fénelon, entrusted with the upbringing of the Grand Dauphin's son, the Duc de Bourgogne, wrote, for the moral, artistic, and political advancement of his pupil, the *Dialogues des Morts*, and *Télémaque*, as well as some *Fables*, somewhat in the style of Perrault. *Télémaque* achieved an enormous and long-enduring popularity, a popularity which has lasted almost to the present day. Courtly old gentlemen of the last generation, elderly colonels and the like, whose schooldays coincided with the earlier half of the nineteenth century, remembered, even if they remembered nothing else, the opening sentences of that famous book : '*Calypso ne pouvait se consoler du départ d'Ulysse. Dans sa douleur elle se trouvait malheureuse d'être immortelle.*' Jules Lemaître says that at school he had to get up long passages by heart in order to recite them in class, but this did not prevent him in maturity from reading and re-reading the book for the pleasure of the thing. Fashions change and in nothing more rapidly and completely

F 69

than in juvenile reading. One might as soon expect to find a boy of to-day engrossed in *Sandford and Merton* as in the *Adventures of Telemachus*, and to-day I gather that *Kidnapped*, and even *Treasure Island*, once universal favourites, are beginning to lose something of their popularity. Lemaître, who picked up *Télémaque* and read it again after forty years and liked it, speaks of its soft and flowery phraseology, that, nevertheless, ' has no colour in it.' Well, if *Télémaque* is dead now, even as a school-book, it scarcely seems just to call it colourless. The landscapes it conjures up to the eye, and the figures that people them, are suggestive of the scenes depicted in old-fashioned mezzo-tints, beautiful indeed, even if a little faded, a little insipid. Yet this work created a prodigious stir in its day ; it enjoyed a popularity perhaps no less wide, and certainly more lasting, than that of d'Urfé's *l'Astrée*, which laid the whole of France under its spell, not only furnishing a universal topic of conversation, but setting the whole tone of social behaviour. Not to have read *l'Astrée*, not to be familiar with the episodes that composed that once enthralling romance, was to write oneself down a barbarian. Alas for the fickleness of popular favour ! *L'Astrée* would be voted quite unreadable to-day. The dust beneath which the romances of Mrs. Radcliffe sleep the morningless and unawakening sleep, is light compared with that which has spread its pall over d'Urfé's one time famous work. So, in a measure, it is with *Télémaque*, nor, in spite of its many beauties, is *Télémaque* likely to be restored to popular favour.

Doubtless, in its day, it owed its renown not wholly to its literary charm. It owed it in no small measure to the glamour which surrounded the person of its author and the sensational controversy in which he played so conspicuous and so tragic a part. Nothing

fails like success ; but failure and misfortune, so
they be in a noble cause and borne with dignity and
resignation, are not seldom a patent to the remem-
brance and veneration of posterity. The name of
Bossuet, the triumphant Bossuet, burns with a very
pale lustre compared with that of Fénelon whom he
helped so effectually to send into exile.

Télémaque consists of eighteen ' books.' As few
are likely to have made acquaintance with it in these
days, it may be well to attempt to summarise the
story.

Things having reached an intolerable pass in
Ithaca, Telemachus makes up his mind to go in
search of his father Ulysses. He sets sail in company
with Mentor, who is none other than Minerva in
disguise. In no long time, a violent storm springs up
and they are cast ashore on the island of Calypso who,
being in high dudgeon at the departure of Ulysses,
extends the most hospitable of welcomes to his son.
Soon she conceives a violent passion for him and
offers to make him immortal if only he will consent
to abide with her. At her request, he tells her the
story of his adventures : How, in Sicily, he had
saved Acestes from an invasion of the barbarians
who, as a mark of his gratitude, had given them a
Phœnician ship to take them home. He narrates
how in Egypt, being compelled to live like a slave
in the desert, he had, on the advice of Termosiris,
the priest of Apollo, instructed the uncouth
shepherds, and taught them milder ways. Then
follow his adventures at Tyre, where he falls into
the power of the cruel Pygmalion, from whom he
escapes in circumstances that scarcely do him credit ;
being condemned to death he escapes with the
connivance of Astarbe, the tyrant's mistress, who
substitutes for Telemachus a young man for whom
she had conceived a passion but who had disdained
her advances. In Cyprus he successfully with-

stands the blandishments of Venus. After a series
of further adventures, he arrives in Crete, where he
gives the people such an admirable explanation of
the laws of Minos that they wish to make him their
king. But Telemachus refuses, preferring poor
Ithaca, *la pauvre Ithaque*, to all the glory and
opulence of Crete. He proposes that they should
choose Mentor, but Mentor also rejects the
proffered honour and, painting a glowing picture of
the virtues of Aristodemus, persuades the Cretans
to choose him for their king. Soon afterwards
Telemachus and Mentor embark on a Cretan
vessel to return to Italy. But Neptune, in order to
soothe the outraged feelings of Venus, raises a
terrible storm which breaks their ship to pieces.
Clinging to fragments of the mast, they are borne
along on the waves, and cast at length on the island
of Calypso. This brings us to the end of the fifth
book. But now, Mentor, in order to save Telemachus from Calypso and Eucharis, plunges him
into the sea. They are picked up by a Phœnician
vessel in which, after a series of incidents too long to
record, they are wafted to Salentum, the city which
is ruled over by Idomeneus. Here at Salentum, with
which the ten remaining books are concerned,
Telemachus learns all that he will need to know
when in after years he will have a kingdom of his own
to rule. Idomeneus was on the point of waging an
unjust war against the Mandurians, but Mentor
contrives to dissuade him, and to bring about a
reconciliation. Thereafter Telemachus throws in his
lot with the Mandurians and their allies against the
wicked Daunians, whose king he slays with his own
hand. In the interval, Mentor has succeeded by a
series of austere but beneficent enactments in
transforming Salentum into an ideal State. At
length, though Idomeneus tries hard to retain them,
they put to sea and arrive, without further adventure,

at Ithaca, where Telemachus finds his father in the
hut of the faithful Eumaeus.

Such, in barest outline, is the story of *Télémaque*.

If *Télémaque* was written for the Duc de Bourgogne, it was not without some shrewd lessons for
the King. In the picture of the ideal ruler whose
lineaments are traced therein, Louis XIV would
have looked in vain for any likeness to himself.
Fénelon energetically denied that he had intended
any reference, oblique or direct, to the King. A
good many people, and the King among them,
thought otherwise.

What then is *Télémaque?* Is it a romance ? An
epic ? A political treatise ? A moral guide ? A
religious tract ? Which of these things is it ? The
answer is : it is all of them together. Its moral and
religious teaching is strictly Christian, but it is
clothed in antique, pagan dress. To begin with, it is,
of course, in its form, and so far as the mere narrative,
the mere story goes, apart, that is to say, from its
political, social, moral, and religious reflections and
exhortations, a work of imitation, though not of
servile imitation. The *Odyssey*, the *Iliad*, the
Aeneid are laid under heavy contribution. Not only
are the various episodes and descriptions clearly
reminiscent, at least in their broad outlines, of those
works of classical antiquity, but we constantly come
upon actual expressions and phrases that are almost
word for word reproductions of those ancient
models.

In these days, as a story of adventure, as a tale
intended for the delectation of the young, it might
seem banal and out-moded (older people would not
fail to find in it a certain faded charm as of old love-
letters laid aside in lavender), but in these days
stories of adventure are no rarities. In Fénelon's
time they were not so common. What would
arouse only a very languid interest in the mind of a

sophisticated youth of to-day, the young Duc de
Bourgogne devoured with zest, eagerly awaiting the
successive developments of a story which, still 'to
be continued,' (it was written in sections, with
lengthy intervals between) held out such promise of
unending entertainment.

As will be seen from the outline of the story which
we have already given, the wanderings of Telemachus
are the wanderings of Ulysses—with variations ;
and Circe is replaced by Calypso. There is, of
course, the inevitable storm, and it bears a striking
resemblance to the storm in the first *Aeneid*. The
contests and games of Virgil faithfully reappear. The
building of Carthage serves as a model for the
building of Salentum. Just as Achilles and Aeneas
had each his shield, Telemachus must needs have
his. Fénelon's description of the Elysian Fields is
based on the sixth *Aeneid*. And so we might continue. And if you would gain any idea of the mode of
life in that Utopian State, Salentum, you will find
plenty of parallels in the *Republic* of Plato.

This is what he says of the King, the true King,
on whose pattern he would mould his royal pupil,
and of the people who have the good fortune to be
his subjects :

' Happy the people that are ruled by a wise king.
They live in happiness and plenty and look with
love upon him to whom they owe their well-being.
It is thus, Telemachus, that you should reign and
compass the welfare of your subjects if it shall please
the gods to bring you into possession of your father's
kingdom. Love your people as if they were your
own children, rejoice in the love they will bear you,
and so order your actions that in enjoying the fruits
of peace and happiness they will always be mindful
of him to whom they owe them. Kings whose sole
aim it is to make themselves feared and to crush
their subjects in order to make them the more humble

and submissive, are the scourges of the human race.
They are feared indeed, as they desire to be, but
they are loathed and detested, and have more to fear
from their subjects than their subjects from them.'

Later on, when Mentor is relating his experiences
in Crete, he thus paints the portrait of a good king :

'He is all-powerful over his people, but the laws
are all-powerful over him. His power to do good is
absolute. But his hands are bound when he would
fain do ill. The laws give him the people in trust as
the most precious thing they can bestow, on condition that he looks upon himself as their father. It
is the gods' will that one man, by his wisdom and
moderation, should work for the felicity of the many,
not that the many, by their misery and servitude,
should flatter the pride and procure the ease and
idleness of one. A king should have no advantage
over others except such as is necessary to bring him
some comfort in his difficult task, or to impress upon
the people the respect due to the upholder of the law.
Indeed the king should live more soberly, less
luxuriously, with less outward magnificence and
pride than others. He should have a fuller measure,
not of riches and pleasures, but of wisdom and
virtue and renown, than the rest of mankind. He
should be the defender of his country and the leader
of her armies abroad, and, at home, the ruler of his
people, so governing them as at all times to bring
them goodness, wisdom, and happiness. Not for
himself did the gods make him king, but that he
might give himself to his people. All his time, all his
care, all his affection he owes to his people, and he
only merits the kingship in so far as he takes no
thought for himself, but devotes himself to the
service of his country.'

Of the Cretan adventure, one of the episodes
describes the Wisdom Contest in which Telemachus
greatly distinguished himself as an interpreter and

expounder of the laws of Minos. The introduction
to this solemn event is impressive :

'Meanwhile the most illustrious and the wisest
among the Cretans conducted us into an ancient and
hallowed wood, withdrawn from the gaze of the
profane, whither the elders, whom Minos had set up
as judges over the people and as guardians of the
laws, had invited us to assemble. We were the same
company as had taken part in the games : no others
were suffered to approach. The sages proceeded to
open the book wherein all the laws of Minos are
gathered together. My heart was filled with awe and
reverence as I drew near to these aged men whose
years had rendered them venerable without depriving
them of their mental vigour. They took their seats
in due order and sat motionless. . . . The most
venerable of these elders opened the book of Laws of
Minos. It was a big book which was ordinarily
kept in a perfumed casket of gold. All the elders
kissed it reverently, for they said that, next to the
gods from whom good laws proceed, nothing could
be more sacred to men than laws intended to make
them good, wise, and happy. Those who had
charge of the laws by which the people were
governed should themselves be obedient to the laws.
Law and not man should rule.' On another page he
says : ' Authority by itself never does any good, it is
not enough that the people should submit. We must
win their hearts.'

Again listen to the words in which Fénelon,
speaking with the tongue of Mentor, sets forth the
doctrine of the Brotherhood of Man :

'Henceforth, under divers names and divers
leaders, you will be but one people. It is thus that
the just gods, who love man, their handiwork,
would be the eternal bond of perfect amity between
them. The whole human race is but one family
spread abroad over the face of the earth. All men

are brothers, and should love one another as brothers.
Woe to those impious ones who seek to win for
themselves a cruel glory by shedding the blood of
their brothers. War is sometimes necessary, it is
true ; but it is the shame of the human race that
sometimes it cannot be avoided. Say not, O ye
kings, that war is the path to glory. True glory is
not to be found apart from human kindness. Whoso
puts his own glory before the dictates of humanity
is a monster of pride, not a man. He will never win
anything but a false glory, for real glory dwells only
in moderation and in kindness. . . . Happy the
king who loves his people and is by them beloved ;
who trusts in his neighbours and they in him, and
who, so far from making war on them, restrains them
from warring among themselves.'

And here, in this picture of a Commonwealth of
States, or, if you will, a League of Nations, he
proclaims the solidarity of the human race :

' Remember then to assemble together from time
to time all ye who govern the mighty cities of
Hesperia. Meet ye together every three years in
general conclave in order that all the kings here
present shall renew their alliance by a fresh oath,
strengthen the covenanted friendship, and take
counsel together on matters of common interest.
So long as you are united you will have peace
within this fair land, and renown and abundance,
and abroad you will always be invincible.'

In the tenth book, the most important of all, he
lays down his scheme for the regeneration of the
world : War is not only wicked, it is unprofitable
even for the victor. Conquest of any kind is
unjust. There must be entire freedom of trade. No
importation of articles calculated to foster luxury
and effeminacy. He prescribes rules regarding food,
dress, the furnishing and adornment of dwelling-
houses. A man is rich, not according to what he

has, but according to what he can do without. As for the makers of luxury goods—not wanted in his ideal state—he would send them back from the town to the country and put them on the land, where they would be perfectly happy with such simple and wholesome cheer as cheeses and chestnuts, evidently the *mitia poma, castaneae molles* and the *pressi copia lactis* which Virgil's Tityrus offered his friend as an inducement to spend the night under his cottage roof. There shall be no vast estates ; a family shall have just as much land as is required to support it. Wine there shall be, but in strict moderation. The state will undertake the education of the children. The shepherds exult and make merry in this happy land. Coridon and Phyllis hasten to the hymeneal altar, the elders weep for joy, raising their trembling hands to heaven.

But if all men are brothers, they are not all equal. Fénelon divides them into seven ranks or classes, (why seven ?) and each class has its distinctive garb, the first, white with a gold fringe at the bottom of their robe. The second, blue ; the third green ; the fourth, saffron ; the fifth, pink ; the sixth, grey ; and the seventh, a combination of yellow and white. He seems to have had an eye for stage effect. In Fénelon's state therefore we have *Liberté*, within bounds ; *Fraternité* ; but not *Egalité*.

Mentor converts the warlike, despotic Idomeneus to the use of a milder and a wiser sceptre. The tone of his remonstrances bears not a little resemblance to that of the letter addressed by Fénelon to Louis XIV. But Fénelon, as we have said, repudiates the suggestion that this book, intended for the edification of the King's grandson, was in any way directed against the King himself. ' *Télémaque*,' he says in a letter to Father Le Tellier, the King's Confessor, ' is a story in the form of an heroic poem, like those of Homer or Virgil, in which I tried to bring in such

teaching as would be beneficial to a young prince who
was one day to succeed to the throne. I wrote it when
I was enjoying the many marks of confidence and
generosity which the King had lavished upon me. I
should surely have proved myself, not only the most
ungrateful, but the most foolish of men, had I
taken occasion to draw un unflattering or ironic
portrait of one to whom I was so indebted. It will
be seen that I deal only in generalities. It is a story
written at high speed and in detached fragments, and
the whole stands in great need of revision.' The
book was written during the years 1693 and 1694;
it was published, in a pirated version and sur-
reptitiously, in 1699, a few months after Fénelon
had been deprived of his duties as a tutor to the
Duc de Bourgogne and of the emoluments attached
to that office. The enemies of Fénelon did not neglect
to use the weapon which seemed to have been thus
providentially put into their hands. The Maréchal
de Noailles, who was anxiously waiting an opportunity to slip into de Beauvilliers' shoes, industriously
sowed the seeds of discord. ' No one,' he said, ' but
the King's sworn enemy could have written such a
thing.' Bossuet not only thought the book un-
becoming in a bishop because of the love-making in
the Eucharis episode, but said that it was obviously
intended as a censure on the King and his ministers.

But this is to anticipate. At the moment, the
horizon, for Fénelon, is brilliant and without a
cloud. He basks in the favour of the most influential
and most reputable section of the Court. The King
may not love him, but he cannot but admire the
genius and graces of *le plus bel esprit*—even if he be
also *le plus chimérique*—of his kingdom. At all
events, he appoints him to the great and wealthy
diocese of Cambrai, still permitting him to retain the
title and emoluments of preceptor to the royal
princes. The path of the future seems strewn with

flowers before him. Yet, even now, secretly, imperceptibly, the forces that are to bring about the ruin of all this glory, the eclipse of all these hopes, are working as yet unguessed at. We are at the turning point in his career, his friendship with Mme Guyon, the famous Quietist controversy, all that long and bitter feud which was soon to send him into perpetual exile.

CHAPTER VIII

OF MYSTICS AND MYSTICISM

BEFORE attempting to deal with Fénelon's mysticism, before essaying to trace the history of his friendship with Mme Guyon and of the momentous consequences which followed therefrom, it may be well to define our terms. What is a mystic ? Few words are more loosely employed. A mystic is often considered in some vague way to be the opposite of a realist, and to call a man a mystic is thus tantamount to calling him a dreamer, a visionary, or, as Louis XIV described Fénelon, *une âme chimérique.* Yet, in point of fact, a mystic is an intense realist, save that what is real to him may seem baseless and illusory to others. ' Do you see nothing there ? ' asks Hamlet of the Queen, and the Queen, believing him bereft of his senses, makes answer : ' Nothing at all, *yet all that is I see.*' What is so terribly real to Hamlet is, for his mother, nothing but the coinage of his brain, the ' bodiless creation ' of ' ecstasy.' ' Alas ! ' she cries, ' he's mad ! '

We often hear writers, particularly poets, referred to as mystical. People are wont to speak of the mystical element in Virgil, for example. What do they mean by this ? Is there any difference in character, any difference, save in the accidental circumstances of time and place, between the *Eclogues* of Virgil and the *Idylls* of Theocritus, for example ? The careless or insensitive observer would say that the former are but imitations, *pastiches,* of the latter. Imitations, in a sense,

indeed they are, but they are a great deal more than
imitations. A new element has crept in, an element
of which we find no trace in the Greek original.
Perhaps that element may be described as the power,
or faculty, of suggesting, consciously or unconsciously, a meaning more profound, more mysterious
than that which the words themselves express. In
Theocritus there is no *hidden* meaning. What he
says, so beautifully and with such grace and charm,
is what he sets out to say : that, and no more than
that. There are no implications, or, as a musician
might put it, no *overtones*. With Virgil it is very
different. There is, in the music of his verse,
superficially so imitative, some subtle quality which
stirs within us ' thoughts beyond the reaches of our
souls,' feelings, emotions, intuitions, mysterious,
incalculable, infinitely variable and quite incapable
of definition. This element of ' other-worldliness '
as we may call it, this sense of something beyond our
sight, this intimation of mystery that haunts the
material world which we perceive with our senses,
this awareness of things unseen, conveyed by some
subtle harmonious cadence, some quite indefinable
collocation of vowel sounds, may be described as
the mystical element in Virgil.

Taking the word then in its widest and most
general sense, we may perhaps say that a mystic is
one who, as he contemplates the material world
around him, is aware, in some mysterious way, of
another, but invisible, world beyond it, a world
infinitely lovelier, infinitely more desirable than the
world he sees. There are those to whom, as to
Newman, ' every breath of air and ray of light and
heat, every beautiful prospect, is, as it were, the
skirts of their garments, the waving of the robes of
those whose faces see God.' For such as these, the
visible creation, the earth, the firmament, nature in
all its infinitely varied manifestations, are as sacra-

mental signs and symbols, economies, adumbrations of the Eternal, dimly shadowing forth something beyond, and infinitely greater than, themselves. ' What we see,' says Newman again, ' is the outward shell of an eternal kingdom ; and on that kingdom we fix the eyes of our faith.' And he goes on to contrast ' this visible world ' with ' that diviner world which as yet we see not.'

Such, too, is the Platonic ideal, the ideal that would have us take delight in whatever is good and lovely in the world we see, yet in such a way as ever to be mindful of that other invisible and eternal world beyond, the home of all perfections, ' which the eyes reach not unto, but faith only.'

In his posthumous work, *Autour de l'Humanisme*, the late Abbé Bremond devotes a section to a consideration of Pascal in relation to the Mystics. In the course of it, he explains and defines mysticism as follows :

' *In eo vivimus et movemur et sumus :* in Him we live and move and have our being. The mystics start with this axiom and we cannot contest their right to do so. Be we good men, or be we evil, Pagan or Christian, God is in us. . . . He is there, not as a thing apart, not, for example, like a prayer-book lying on the bottom of a cupboard, but as the living principle of all life. He is not present as an idea, for, whether it be intuitive or inferential, the *idea* of God is not God. We are (he continues) all potential mystics. We become actual ones as soon as we attain to any sort of consciousness of God within us ; as soon as we make any sort of test of His presence ; as soon as this contact . . . becomes recognisable to us, and takes on the character of an encounter, an embrace, a possessing.' These are mystics in the stricter sense of the word, for they have had experience of God within them, of God indwelling, or immanent, in their inmost being.

But there are those also of whom it were more accurate to say that they are *tinged* with mysticism, that they have a tendency towards mysticism, rather than that they are mystics. Such persons are imbued with a kind of vague spiritual nostalgia, a longing for that other world of which they have caught, or dream they have caught, a faint and fleeting glimpse. ' It may be,' says Bremond, ' and for my part I am almost persuaded that it is so, that in the feeblest prayer, nay, in the slightest æsthetic emotion, there is the trace of an experience of the same order, mystical even at that stage, but imperceptible, evanescent.'

' It is,' Abbé Bremond continues, ' when they attempt to describe their experience' (i.e. what he calls the ' encounter,' the ' embrace,' the ' possessing') ' that the mystics find themselves of necessity in a considerable dilemma. For lack of better means, they are compelled to adopt, in order to express their mystical experiences, words and phrases commonly employed to describe the impressions which external, tangible things habitually make upon us. They talk of " heat," " taste," " feeling," and so on, warning us, however, that these words are not to be taken in their literal sense. God is not a flame, nor a fruit. He is not something we can feel and handle. Sometimes they take their metaphors from the sphere of the mind, of the intellect, and talk of their " illuminations," their " certitudes." In either case, mystical contemplation, mystical knowledge, is as remote from rational knowledge, which is arrived at by a process of ratiocination upon intellectual concepts, as it is from knowledge attained by way of the senses (sight, touch, etc.). The knowledge of the mystic is knowledge, indeed, but it is indeterminate, indefinite. It is the result of contact, as in the case of knowledge gained through the senses, but the contact in this case is the contact of spirit with spirit.

' The opponents of mysticism ask, not without some *prima facie* justification, what is the use of this vague, indeterminate, indefinite knowledge, and why it should be preferred to knowledge that is clear and sharply defined ? Why, in religion, or in anything else, prefer the vague, the obscure, the indefinite to that which stands out before our eyes in bold and unmistakable relief ? Is not this, they ask, " the very essence of obscurantism ? " To such a question there can be but one answer. Obviously, to adopt such a preference would be more than unreasonable, it would be immoral. But, in point of fact, the mystics do no such thing. They do not prefer the vague to the clear, or rate the indefinite higher than the definite. They compare not one *idea* with another *idea ;* but—and this is a very different thing—one mode of knowledge with another mode of knowledge. Their concern is not with ideas and deductions from ideas, their concern is with reality. To knowledge based on reason, to knowledge which proceeds from ideas and which, therefore, is the more perfect in proportion as those ideas are clear and definite, they oppose the knowledge of personal experience, very mysterious yet very real, which, germinating at the soul's core, fuses it, not to an idea of God, but to God Himself. This differentiation between two modes of knowledge, or rather of knowing, contains the whole secret of mysticism.'

But these two modes of knowing are not rivals ; rather are they complementary, one of the other. ' The mystics,' Bremond proceeds, ' do not set up their inward experience in opposition to intellectual knowledge, as if the one were the enemy of the other. . . . In its proper sphere—forming concepts, comparing, reasoning, constructing—the understanding, the intellect, is excellent and wholly without reproach. Both modes of knowing reach out to the

same object, but they do so each in its own special
manner. The one aims at knowing the truth *about*
God, the other at knowing God Himself. The
knowledge in the one case is notional ; in the other,
real. But it is one and the same soul which has a
core and a surface, which reasons about God, and
which possesses Him.' Finally—and this, as we
shall see, is the answer to Bossuet and the rest who
would charge Fénelon with encouraging, or at least
condoning, a neglect of the sacraments—Bremond
concludes thus : ' The mystic is not content with
possessing God ; he aims, and, lest he should sink
beneath the quicksands of Quietism, he is bound to
aim, at making the whole of his superficial being,
that is to say of his thinking and voluntary being,
share in this possession and make it its own, submitting himself by acts of admiration and love to the
Divine Presence.'

It has been authoritatively stated that Fénelon's
doctrine of mysticism, as it is developed in his successive writings on the subject, is open to serious objection. According to Cherel, the *gravamen* of the
criticism directed against it is that it fails to present
any clear distinction between mystical prayer proper,
and Christian prayer in general. In order that the
soul may enter upon a state of mystical prayer,
special divine graces are necessary, and these are
called the mystical graces. Now, it appears that,
although we may prepare ourselves for the reception
of these graces and co-operate in their action, we
cannot by any conscious exercise of our will put ourselves in a state of mystical prayer, nor can we be
sure that, as a result of any preparation on our part,
the necessary mystical graces will be vouchsafed to
us. In none of his writings, says Cherel, does
Fénelon make this distinction clear. True, he says
that preparation for the mystical state consists in
practising ' self-abandonment ' ; true, also, that he

speaks of ' elect souls ' to whom God grants the privilege of the mystical state, referring to what he calls the ' freedom of God ' (*la liberté de Dieu*) in the distribution of His gifts, by which, presumably, he means to say that God bestows or withholds His divine gifts according to His sovereign and inscrutable will.   It is when we come to examine Fénelon's writings *in extenso* and in their due order that there appears to emerge the notion that, whoso does not love God as the mystics love Him, is not merely one from whom God has seen fit to withhold the mystical graces, but one who himself deliberately incurs the blame of preferring a lower to a higher form of prayer, of setting the imperfect above the perfect. That he is not a mystic, is, in a word, to be regarded, not as a misfortune over which he has no control, but as a deliberate moral delinquency.   The fact that the theological virtue of hope is ' selfish,' grieves and perplexes Fénelon.   He hesitated, he confessed, to sign Article IX of the Issy conferences, wherein it is declared : ' It is not permissible for a Christian to be indifferent to his own salvation.'   In his eyes, the world of morals, and of natural and supernatural virtue, is divided into two parts—on the one side, *self-interest ;* on the other, *selflessness*. The one perverse, unjust, and false ; the other, good and in conformity with the desires (*goûts*) of God and man.

This identification, or fusion, of the desires of God and man, was the principal clause in the indictment of the Quietist error.   God, by the mystical graces which He bestows, brings to the soul when it responds and clings thereto in moments of prayer, or contemplation, or ' union,' an extraordinary sensation of infinity and divine plenitude, a complete detachment from self, a pliant and perfect abandonment to all the movements of grace ; in short, He suspends, in the elect soul, all perceptible activity.

Such are the results, the divine results, of mystical prayer. But that which is an *effect* of mystical perfection, the Quietists are fain to consider and employ as a *means* to attain it. Without waiting for the coming of the mystical graces, they deliberately banish or neglect every distinct view of the attributes of God, of the Divine Persons, of Our Lord Jesus Christ. Not content with mortifying self-love within them, as it behoves every Christian to do, they blame, both in themselves and others, all pursuit of happiness, whether temporal or eternal ; and, under pretext of rendering themselves amenable to the divine promptings, arrest and condemn all activity of the soul. Such is the *Moyen Court*, or ' Short Way,' by which they claim to arrive at perfection. Abbé de Gosselin, a learned and saintly Sulpician, who published and edited the definitive edition of Fénelon's works, has drawn out the points wherein the false mystics have misrepresented and distorted the principles and tendencies of the true. He sets them forth in a series of five paragraphs as follows :

(1) The true mystics teach that the act of contemplation, that is to say, the simple and loving attentiveness to the presence of God, may last for periods varying with the disposition of the contemplative soul, and, especially, with the strength of the grace which draws it on to contemplation. The false mystics hold that it can last for years, and even for a lifetime, without any need to renew it. Such a notion of perfection is chimerical, and incompatible with the frailty of our nature.

(2) The true mystics teach that, in mystical contemplation, the love with which we look upon God is an act of pure charity, which believeth all things, hopeth all things, suffereth

all things and asketh all things (St. Paul). It
contains, in a pre-eminent degree, all the acts
of religion, though it does not dispense us from
the obligation of performing them in more
express fashion at the proper season. The false
mystics hold on the contrary, and it evidently
follows from the principles they profess concerning the perpetual and uninterrupted contemplation of the perfect, that these latter are
dispensed from all explicit and distinct acts of
charity, from all reflecting on themselves and on
the truths of religion ; and, consequently, that
such acts and such reflecting are only appropriate to neophytes and to the imperfect.

(3) True mystics teach that the most perfect
contemplation is that which looks upon the
Divine Nature in its most abstract and general
aspects, such as those of Being, of Truth, of
Perfection, but they recognise at the same time
that any object of faith may be an object of
contemplation. The false mystics, on the
contrary, seem to hold that the only true object
of contemplation is that which attaches to God
alone. They go further and affirm that this
general and indivisible contemplation of God
is the sole, perpetual act of the perfect
contemplative.

(4) In the language of the true mystics, holy
indifference and entire abandonment to God's
pleasure, even amid the most grievous trials, is
to be interpreted only as not desiring anything
save for the glory of God and in conformity
with His holy will. False mystics, on the
contrary, go so far as to exclude absolutely all
desire for salvation and all co-operation of the
soul in the inspirations of grace.

(5) True mystics teach that amid the trials
of the interior life, the lower part of the soul is

separated from the higher in the sense that the imagination and the senses may be troubled by temptations, without the understanding and the will taking any part in them. They add, however, that the separation can never be complete and that there always remains a sufficient link between the two parts for it to be necessary that the higher should control the lower and repress its unlawful motions. False mystics, on the other hand, assert that in perfect souls the separation between the two parts is complete and absolute, so that whatever irregularity takes place in the lower part, cannot be imputed as a sin to the higher.

Such are the characteristics of true mysticism as contra-distinguished from the false. It must not be assumed that the tenets of either Fénelon or Mme Guyon wholly coincided with what is here described as 'false mysticism.' Very far from it. We have seen where Fénelon is said to have erred, namely in not sufficiently distinguishing between mystical or contemplative prayer and Christian prayer in its ordinary and general sense. Mme Guyon would certainly have repudiated with all the energy at her command the pernicious doctrine (the doctrine of Molinos) attributed to the false mystics in paragraph five above quoted. Her teaching may be summed up briefly as follows :

(1) Human perfection is attainable even in this life, and consists in one continual act of contemplation and love, which act contains in itself all the acts of religion. Once attained, it is indefectible and ends not, unless it is expressly revoked.

(2) A soul which has attained perfection is no longer obliged to perform any explicit, distinct acts of charity.

(3) In this state of perfection, the soul should be indifferent to everything, whether for the body or the soul, and whether temporal or eternal.

(4) When in a state of perfect contemplation, the soul should reject all distinct ideas, even the thought of the attributes of God and the mysteries of Jesus Christ.

A comparison of her teaching as thus summarised, with the true mysticism as set forth above, will show where Mme Guyon erred and also perhaps make clear that her errors were chiefly errors of over-statement and exaggeration. The act of contemplation and love is not indefectible, it does not last for ever without renewal. It does not, therefore, dispense us from the due observance in their proper season of our religious duties. Nor is it permitted to man to be indifferent to his eternal salvation. As for Fénelon, he expressly condemns in his *Maximes* the *continuous* act of love and contemplation as put forward by the false mystics ; but he makes perfection consist in an habitual state of pure love in which desire of reward and fear of punishment have no part. ‘ *Cambrai*,’ the Pope is said to have remarked, ‘ *pèche par excès d’amour divin, et Meaux par défaut d’amour pour le prochain.*’ ‘ Cambrai ’ may also have erred by too much *finesse*, by an excess of dialectical subtlety. Mme de Grignan once asked Bossuet if Fénelon really had as much *esprit* as people said he had. ‘ *Ah, Madame ! il en a à faire peur !* ’ was the reply.

In regard to a subject so delicate and beset with so many pitfalls as this of Mysticism, it were prudent to have recourse to an unimpeachable authority. I, therefore, take from a work entitled *The English Mystics*, an account of what its author, Dom David Knowles, calls ‘ the normal Catholic view of the matter, which view ' he says, ' in spite of controversy on points of detail, is taught in theory and practice by theologians and directors throughout the world to-day, and which has been extracted as a system from the writings of holy souls throughout the Christian ages ' :

> ' The God ' (says this writer) ' who is the object of our love and service is invisible to our senses and incomprehensible to our intellect. All our knowledge of him is derived from a process of abstraction and reasoning either from what we know of his creatures or from what he himself has revealed to us of himself— that is, in the light of unassisted reason or of reason aided by faith. When we pray to God, we direct our minds to a personality represented in our minds by a very complex concept or idea ; the work of our reason and imagination working upon the material supplied by senses and imagination. We certainly believe, as Christians, that we have received supernatural habits and capabilities by the gifts of the Holy Ghost, and that we are constantly receiving sufficient supernatural grace or assistance to give our actions merit to eternal life, but we do not im- mediately perceive our reception of this grace any more than we immediately perceive the existence of God.
>
> ' In heaven, on the other hand, we shall see God as he is, and his action upon our souls will be felt immediately. Between this condition and that in which we live here below, there is clearly room for many intermediate states, such, for instance, as was that of the angelic intelligences during their time of trial, and it is the common view of Catholic theologians that mystics—that is, those expert in contemplative

prayer—have in some part gone forward towards the Beatific Vision. Their finite concept of God, purified from association with creatures and simplified as far as may be, has in some degree given place to an apprehension of God, not yet seen as he is in the Beatific Vision, but yet approaching to that Vision. Their realisation of God's action on the soul is no longer the work of a reasoned process starting from the truths of revelation ; they perceive it immediately, so that it seems to them that he alone is acting and that they and their will are altogether passive. Hence the name of Passive Union has been given to some moments of contemplative prayer. Very often, alternatively, God may act directly on the intellect—that is, without any precedent activity of senses or imagination—and infuse new knowledge of supernatural truth, either contained in ordinary revelation or not.

' The mystical experience, therefore, is a development of the action of grace. It is a *gratia gratum faciens*, a grace ordained by God for the further sanctification of the soul, and indeed the great mystics are unanimous in maintaining that the mystical experience purifies the soul more than years of mortification could do. It takes place only in a soul at peace with God and, ordinarily speaking, advanced in holiness, but mystics and theologians reiterate that the ultimate criterion of a soul's worth before God is not the degree of mystical favour received, but the degree of charity inherent in the soul, and that the charity of one who is not a contemplative may be greater than the charity of a mystic. It is entirely supernatural, though not necessarily miraculous, and is a growth, whether ordinary or extraordinary, of the normal supernatural life present, at least in germ, in every soul in a state of grace. Thus the only true mystics, in the Catholic sense of the word, belong to the Church of Christ, though they may well belong to the soul, and not to the body, of that Church. The hand of the Lord is not straitened, that he should not save, and just as we can never say that a particular soul within the visible Church has greater charity than one without, so we have no reason to suppose that the favours of contemplative prayer may not be given to those of good will who are ordained to die outside the pale of the visible Church.'[1]

[1] *The English Mystics*, by Dom David Knowles (pp. 31–33), London, Burns Oates & Washbourne, 1927.

CHAPTER IX

MADAME GUYON

JEANNE MARIE BOUVIÈRES DE LA MOTHE, the *femme fatale* of Fénelon's career, was born at Montargis, on April 13, 1648. She was thus three years his senior.

It would be easy—as Bossuet was soon to discover—to belittle Mme Guyon, to hold her up to mockery and ridicule. The thoughtless, or the profane, nay, even the honest Philistine, would find in her deeds and in her writings abundant occasion for satire. An alienist of to-day would probably describe Mme Guyon's spiritual experiences as hallucinations, and ascribe them to hysteria or insanity. In point of fact, Mme Guyon was a woman of remarkable mental and spiritual endowments, and of extraordinary personal charm.

Nevertheless, it cannot be denied that there was a marked strain of morbidity in her composition. She was an eight months child ; her mother, when nearing her term, had brought her forth prematurely in consequence of a fright. Eight months children, if they live at all, are usually delicate. Mme Guyon was no exception to the rule. While she was still a little child, she suffered from a tumour at the base of the spine. This was followed by an ulcer—described as 'gangrenous'—which appeared, first on one thigh, and then on the other. When she was five, she began to have visions, and developed a strain of precocious religious enthusiasm. She eagerly listened to stories of the saints, notably of St. Teresa, in whose footsteps she longed to follow. Then, a year or two later, she read about St. Francis de Sales, and Mme de Chantal. She was not yet in her teens when she made up her mind to become a nun, and importuned her mother to put her with the Visitandines. Her mother declined, on the ground that, her father being away, she could not take upon herself the responsibility of agreeing to so grave a step. Not to be put off, the child forged a letter, purporting to come from her mother, entreating the nuns to receive her. But the Mother Superior was not deceived. The subterfuge, it is not surprising to learn, was straightway detected.

Some two years later, she underwent an experience which, for the time being, totally eclipsed her religious ardour. She was taken by her father on a journey into the country. With them went a very accomplished young gentleman, a kinsman. The young people were mutually attracted, but her father frowned on the proceedings, and the courtship was nipped in the bud. Instead of quickening her desire for the cloister, this abortive love-affair diverted her thoughts to the world, and its allurements. She grew immeasurably vain, and spent whole hours in front of her looking-glass, adorning and admiring herself. She became careless about her prayers, and before long omitted them altogether. Fortune—or misfortune—took her to Paris, where she attracted much attention. And no wonder! Her eyes, it is said, were marvellous, her nose beautifully moulded, her mouth bewitching, her hands small and shapely. She danced, she coquetted, she steeped herself in pleasure, she delighted in tales of love and chivalry. Her dream was short-lived. She was no more than sixteen when, at the instigation of her parents, she entered into a *mariage de convenance* with one Jacques Guyon, a man twenty-two years her senior, who had nothing but his wealth—and that was considerable—to recommend him. No sooner had she entered her husband's house, than a feeling of *ennui*, of hopelessness, descended upon her like a pall. Not only were her husband's manners rough and morose, but there was in the house another inmate, one who could not be ignored ; this was her mother-in-law, who took an immediate dislike to her, and was at no pains to conceal it.

Mme Guyon bore her husband five children in ten years ; but motherhood brought no consolation to her lonely spirit. Instead of diminishing her woes, it added to them, for two of her children were carried away by smallpox. How was she to find courage to bear the long and cheerless years that lay before her ? Whither should she turn ? Where should she look, if not for help, at least for solace ? It was now, when the world had failed her, when its pleasures had turned to ashes in her mouth, when she could not go abroad, and met with nothing but coldness or hostility at home, when there was nothing to refresh and water the desert of her existence—it was now that she turned again to the religion she had practised as a child. The martyrdom for which she then had craved, seemed likely to be hers, but without the martyr's glory. The years were fleeting by. Of whom should she seek that love for which her heart so long and eagerly had hungered—of whom, if not of God ? But God withheld Himself from her, and hid His face. Long, long she sought Him, with prayer and penance, subjecting her flesh to incredible and, sometimes, revolting mortifications. In vain. The skies were empty ! There was none to hear.

More than one to whom she had unburdened her troubles, and whom she had made the confidants of her religious perplexities, had spoken to her of what they mysteriously called the inward life, *la vie intérieure.* But these words brought no illumination to her mind. They meant nothing to her. A cousin of hers, a missionary lately returned from Cochin-China, had told her too of some strange mode of prayer in which he ' thought of nothing,' but what this meant, what it could possibly mean, she, excusably enough, had not the faintest apprehension. For long she remained as one groping in the darkness, with no sign to guide her. Then, quite suddenly, the heavens opened.

Was it chance, or the secret workings of Providence that brought her into contact with another man of religion to whom, once more, she explained her religious perplexities, more especially her difficulty regarding prayer ? God was for her but a name, an abstraction. How and where should she seek Him ? And immediately, he made answer, saying : ' Madame, you are looking outside for that which is within you. Make up your mind to seek God in your heart, and you shall surely find Him.'

Those words went through her ' like an arrow.' They pierced her through and through. ' Straightway,' she wrote, ' I was conscious of a very deep wound ; yet a wound full of sweetness and of love ; a wound so sweet that I longed never to be healed of it.'

And so after long and fruitless searching, she had found what she sought, within her own heart. *Foris Te quærebam et intus eras.*

It was soon after she had been visited by this sudden and startling illumination that, through the medium of Père de La Mothe, her brother, who was Superior of the Order of Barnabites in Paris, she became acquainted with Père La Combe, a member of the same community. It was an acquaintance which, on each side, grew, with the swiftness of fire, into a kind of spiritual infatuation, which was the undoing of both. For her it ended in loss of friends,

MME GUYON

calumny, exile ; for him in the long-drawn torture of imprisonment, madness, and the grave.

Père La Combe had been proposed to her as her director. In point of fact it was she, not he, who from the outset assumed that office. 'We spoke together a little,' she says, describing their first interview. ' By God's grace I was enabled to say words which revealed to him the mystery of the inner life.' He departed from her, as he afterwards confessed, ' a new man.'

He was thirty-one when this meeting took place, and she but twenty-three. Nine years were to elapse before they saw each other again ; but neither time nor distance availed to dim the memory of that first encounter. They did not forget. Those intervening years were tragic ones for her. In a single day she lost her father and a little girl. And at last, after twelve years of loveless wedlock, her husband died. Nevertheless, for years after this she continued to endure unutterable anguish of mind and spirit.

On July 22, in the year 1680, peace suddenly filled her heart. That day, Père La Combe, saying his Mass at Thonon, had a revelation which, it seems, he hastened to make known to her whom it concerned, for Mme Guyon thus records it. ' As he offered me to God at the first *memento*, an inner voice spoke to him very clearly, saying : '' Ye shall dwell together in the same place.'' He marvelled greatly thereat, for never until then had he heard an inner voice.'

Deeming this a mandate she dared not disobey, she betook herself, accompanied by her youngest child, a little girl of five, to Geneva, with whose Bishop, M. d'Arcanthon, she was acquainted. There had been some talk of founding a branch house of *les Nouvelles Catholiques* at Gex, and to the furtherance of that scheme she had given all the money at

her disposal. Thither came Père La Combe, and
so, after nine sundering, but not estranging, years,
they met again, and entered on that strange association which was to lead them, through suspicion,
ridicule and calumny, to irretrievable disaster.

'As soon as I saw the Father'—thus she described
the meeting—'I was amazed to feel an inward grace
such as I had never before experienced. It was as
though an emanation proceeded from him to me,
through the most intimate channels of the spirit,
and it seemed to return from me to him, so that he
was conscious of the same effect. There was,' she
adds, 'nothing human or earthly in our union.'

Just as there is a 'marriage of true minds,' may
there not also be a marriage of souls, the nuptials
of the spirit ? Hear this epithalamium of unincarnate
union :

'I gradually came to perceive, when Père La
Combe entered to hear my confession, or to give me
Holy Communion, that I could no longer speak to
him in words, and that there was produced, within
the depths of my being, the same silence that came
over me when I thought of God. I understood it
to be God's will that I should realise that, even in
this life, men may learn to speak with the language
of angels. It was thus that we understood one another
in God, in a way that was wholly ineffable and
divine. Our hearts spoke to one another and
communicated a grace no words can tell. This
was a new country for him and for me, but divine
beyond expression.'

One night, at Turin, a dream came to Mme
Guyon :

'There was a great mountain at the foot of which
was a stormy sea, studded with reefs. Above this
mountain, towered another mountain encompassed
about with hedges, and it had a lock and key. The
Master came and opened the door to let me in. And

immediately it was closed again. The Master was
none other than the Bridegroom who, taking me
by the hand, led me into a wood which was all of
cedars. This mountain was called Mount Lebanon.
Within the wood was a chamber, to which the
Bridegroom led me, and in the chamber were two
beds. I asked him for whom these two beds were
intended, and he answered me, saying : " One is
for my Mother and the other, my Bride, for thee ! "
There were wild creatures in this room, creatures
of contrary natures, who dwelt together in wondrous
contentment. The cat played harmlessly with the
bird, and pheasants came and caressed me ; the wolf
and the lamb dwelt together in amity. I remembered
the prophecy of Isaias, and of the chamber whereof
it is spoken in the Canticle. . . . The Bridegroom
said to me : " I have chosen thee, my Bride, in
order to draw unto thee all who shall have courage
to cross that dreadful sea ! "

What was the message of this dream if not to tell
her that she was specially beloved of Christ, that it
was her task to go forth and renew the Church and
the world by teaching the gospel of pure love ?
And so she sets out with Père La Combe to fulfil her
supernatural mission. What candour, what childlike innocence ! But, also, what an occasion for
calumny ! And, indeed, slander, and ridicule and
indignant hostility were their portion in most
abundant measure. She renounced her property,
nearly all of it, in her children's favour, retaining for
herself just sufficient to supply her barest needs.
There is no doubting her purity and sincerity, let
the scoffers hint or say what they may. Mad she
may have seemed, or what the world calls mad.
Unbalanced, perhaps, indeed, she was. But she
was passionately in earnest. Though many sneered
and scoffed, many, too, were carried away by the

H

tempestuous eloquence of her words. She had her
disciples in every grade of society, and chiefly among
the highest. Persecuted and slandered, bemocked,
and ridiculed, she continued her crusade with
unwearying ardour. On her, she deemed, was laid
a mandate to renew the world and the Church,
and love, *le pur amour*, was the means that had been
revealed to her.

It is casting no suspicion on the character of her
relations with Père La Combe to say that they were
exceedingly embarrassing to her friends and well-
wishers. It is at least possible that, without that
association and the scandal to which it gave rise, the
ecclesiastical authorities might have left her unmolested. As it was, the first steps taken against her
were disciplinary rather than doctrinal.

It happened, strangely enough, that Mme Guyon's
own brother was none other than that Père La Mothe
who ruled over the House of the Barnabites in Paris
with such exemplary good sense and moderation.
That one of his own monks should behave with such
extravagance would in itself have been a source of
grave annoyance to him; that his aider and abettor
in this scandalous business should be none other
than his own sister, was beyond endurance. He tried
by every means in his power to persuade her to
return to Montargis. In vain. She refused to listen
for a moment to his entreaties. But the strain was
beginning to tell upon her. It looked for a time
as though she would lose her reason. She began
to exhibit signs of delusional insanity. She thought
everyone was against her. Her own brother, the
Provincial of the Barnabites, was (she averred)
certainly conspiring to ruin La Combe. Forgery,
lies, trumped-up charges, false witness, blackmail
—these she said were some of the vile weapons
employed with the connivance—nay, with the
approval—of the high ecclesiastical authorities

to involve both her and her companion in disgrace.

At last her conduct did indeed bring about the thing which she had prophesied. She and La Combe were jointly proceeded against as persons suspected of holding—and propagating—the pernicious opinions of the once exalted, but now discredited, Molinos. La Combe's *Analysis of Mental Prayer* and Mme Guyon's *Moyen Court* were the works cited as containing the reprehensible doctrine. The case against them being regarded as proven, both the accused were called upon to sign a retractation. Both refused. La Combe was immediately shut up in the Bastille. He did not remain there long. Dragged about from prison to prison, suffering every kind of mental torture, he was at last incarcerated in the Château de Lourdes, and at last, completely bereft of his senses, he came to the end of his restless and unhappy existence.

Despite the mountains of ridicule and insult that have been heaped upon his memory, Père La Combe seems to have been a man of uncommon mental gifts. It is true he was mad when he died, but that is not surprising, considering the tortures which he had had to go through. He was a man of parts as well as an enthusiast but, like many other enthusiasts, he was occasionally betrayed into words and actions that were both exaggerated and absurd. He lays down, for example, that the excellent gift of contemplation has often been vouchsafed, not only to rude, uneducated people, to ignorant peasant women, but even to little boys and girls of four years old. He recommends several kinds of prayer, the prayer of simplicity, of childlike faith, of silence and meditation, of the presence of God, and finally of *sleep*, which he declares to be the ultimate perfection, the pure essence of prayer !

Mme Guyon, being in ill health, was allowed to

remain at large some three months longer than her
companion. They may have thought separation
would aid persuasion. If they did, they were wrong.
It hardened her resistance.

On January 29, 1688, the Eve of the Feast of St.
Francis de Sales, Mme Guyon was conveyed to the
Convent of the Visitandines, passing as a prisoner
into the very place she had aspired in her childhood
to enter as a postulant. Then, and not for the first
time, she wrought a miracle. Such was her grace,
her charm, her gentleness, that she captivated her
captors—the nuns were completely won over by her.

In the world without, her friends did not desert
her. They looked on her as a saintly woman
grievously misunderstood and cruelly maltreated.
'All her women friends,' says Voltaire, ' were loudly
indignant that M. de Harlay, who notoriously cared
too much for women, should persecute a woman
who only cared for God.'

The captivity of Mme Guyon did not last long.
Her friends were influential and they did not
slumber. Owing to the united efforts of Mme de
Maisonfort, her first cousin, of the warm-hearted
Mme de Miramion, and, lastly, of no less a person
than Mme de Maintenon, the prisoner regained her
freedom. Certainly, she signed some kind of a
retractation ; but this she afterwards repudiated.

She wrote to Mme de Maintenon expressing
gratitude for her intervention. She followed up her
letter with a visit to St. Cyr. The letter had given
Mme de Maintenon a most favourable impression
of the writer. That impression was abundantly
fulfilled when she saw the writer herself. Mme de
Maintenon received her most graciously, and she,
too, fell beneath the spell—for a time. Mme
Guyon became *persona grata—gratissima* in fact—
at St. Cyr, among the teachers as well as among the
taught.

CHAPTER X

THE BATTLE OPENS

'O TRUTH, O Light, we see but by Thee alone; yet few are they who see Thee and know Thee, what Thou art. The objects of Nature men behold through Thee alone, yet they doubt Thy existence. In the light of Thy rays men discern all the creatures that exist; yet they doubt whether Thou shinest. Thou shinest, indeed, in the darkness; but the darkness knoweth Thee not, and refuseth to know Thee. O gentle Light, happy is he who beholdeth Thee! Happy, I say, through Thee, for Thou art the Truth and the Life. Whosoever seeth Thee not is blind. Nay, worse; he is dead. Give me, therefore, eyes to see Thee and henceforth Thee alone. If I see Thee, all I need is mine. I am satisfied to the full as soon as Thou appearest.'

Fénelon, when he wrote those words, was assuredly not far away in spirit from her who adjures us ' to study ceaselessly to lose all will of our own in the will of God; to renounce all private inclinations, how good soever they may seem, as soon as we feel them coming into being, in order to put ourselves in a state of indifference, and only to will what God has willed from all Eternity; to be indifferent to all things, whether of the body or of the soul, to our temporal or eternal welfare, to leave the past in oblivion, the future to Providence, and the present to God . . . to look on all things in God, and to look on them as coming infallibly from His hand, saving only our sins.'

'The God of the Christian people,' says Pascal, 'is a God who makes the soul feel that He is her only good, that her only rest is in Him, that her only joy is in loving Him; and who makes her at the same time abhor the obstacles which keep her back and prevent her from loving God with all her strength.'

It is thus that Mme Guyon gives her soul to God. She bids us resign ourselves unstintingly, unreservedly to this Power within us, to love and adore it simply without thought of reward or punishment, without regard for self. When we have identified ourselves completely with this power, when we have thoroughly achieved the conquest of self and live in this power, we are spiritually perfect.

But this doctrine of pure love, of love absolute, infinite, unlimited and unconditional, the love in which we surrender ourselves, heart and soul and will, to the will of the Beloved, loving Him with no thought of ourselves, asking no reward, no recompense, heedless of what may become of us hereafter, brings, or may bring, some dangerous sequels in its train. This Quietism, so all-sufficient, all-embracing, tends to diminish the importance of religious practice, to seem to render superfluous the observance of our religious duties and to lead even to the neglect of the sacraments.

Mme Guyon, with Fénelon as her advocate, won over Mme de Maintenon to her cause, and the conquest of Mme de Maintenon meant the conquest of Saint-Cyr. Mme de Maintenon had been born and bred a Huguenot. Was it, then, something in the simplicity, the freedom, the directness of this new approach to God, appealing to some lingering remnants of the Protestant in her, that captivated Mme de Maintenon? Or was it merely the attraction of novelty?

Sometime in 1690, Fénelon writes to Mme de Maintenon a letter in which he sets forth at length the doctrine of pure love, that is to say, of love involving the complete abandonment of self, love given with no thought of recompense from the Beloved, love utterly uncalculating and disinterested.

'The more you die to yourself,' says he, 'by abandoning everything to the spirit of God, the more you will have it in your heart to bear with the faults of others and to regard them with unlimited compassion. On every hand you will behold but wretchedness. Your sight will be more penetrating and you will see more of it than you see to-day. But nothing will scandalize you, or surprise you, or cause you to shrink into yourself. You will behold corruption in man, even as you behold water in the ocean.

'The world is lax, but the world is pitiless. You will bear no resemblance to the world. You will be faithful and exact in your duties ; but compassionate and gentle as was Jesus Christ towards sinners, as when He rebuked the Pharisees, whose outward virtues were so conspicuous.'

At Saint-Cyr, we are told : 'The whole house, almost, became Quietist without knowing it. No one talked of anything save of the pure love of God, of self-abandonment, of holy indifference, of simplicity. This last-named virtue served as a veil for all their little self-indulgences. They treated themselves to their little comforts with the holy liberty of the children of God. No one worried about anything, not even about their salvation.'

Suddenly the wind changed. Someone, namely the Bishop of Chartres, who happened to be the ecclesiastical superior of Saint-Cyr, told Mme de Maintenon that matters must not go on as they were. In a trice Mme Guyon and Fénelon were dropped.

And now, what did Fénelon do ? He decided on a bold step. Perhaps, not seeing its possible consequences, he did not think it bold. Perhaps—such was his candour and such, we may add, his belief in Mme Guyon—he thought it perfectly natural.

Outwardly, at any rate, his relations with Bossuet were still as friendly and affectionate as they had ever been. But he knew that an undercurrent of coolness had recently made itself felt between them. The Eagle of Meaux had begun to look askance on his association with Mme Guyon. Fénelon, therefore, who hated anything like double-dealing, or concealment, resolved to be perfectly open. He prevailed on Mme Guyon to submit her theories and her books to Bossuet. This, he deemed, would at least bear witness to her *bona fides*, and to his. Why should he not take such a step ? What had he to fear ? As to the soundness of his case, he had no doubt of it.

Mme Guyon needed no great amount of persuasion. She was not unaware of her powers. That same charm and fascination which had brought so many others—Fénelon, even Mme de Maintenon—under her spell, would not be lost on Bossuet. Thus she thought. She was soon undeceived.

Bossuet was indeed the last man in the world to weigh the merits of such a case. The Eagle of Meaux represented commonsense magnified to an heroic scale ; he stands for mediocrity in all its majesty ; in him we behold the apotheosis of the ordinary. He marched with an honest, rotund magnificence along the appointed highway of salvation. For spiritual novelties, religious nostrums he had little time and less taste. *Quod semper, quod ubique quod omnibus* was in a very special sense his motto. He was by this time on the threshold of old age. The burden of his sixty-six years, and of a multiplicity of tasks, was a heavy one. But if he could strike a blow for the Church and the cause of orthodoxy, he was the last man to shrink from the

task proposed to him, however little he might relish
it. This new-fangled system of praying was gaining
ground, becoming modish. It was high time some
firm stand was made against this perilous *nirvana*,
alluring as a mirage, treacherous as a quicksand. He
therefore went to pay Mme Guyon a preliminary
visit at her house. M. de Chevreuse was present at
the interview.

The interview could not have passed off with
greater civility and politeness. There was nothing
in the nature of a discussion. Mme Guyon promised
to send him all her works, whether printed or in
manuscript, and Bossuet undertook to read them in
his country house at Germigny. He should need,
he said, four or five months for the task. All that
time she gave him no rest. She bombarded him
with letters, notes and explanations, assuring him
continuously of her duty, and of her eagerness in all
things to defer to his ruling.

Bossuet, in the peace of his rural retreat, sat down
to his task ; a formidable one indeed ! Bossuet was
himself very little of a mystic. So far from
endeavouring to conceal his ignorance of the subject,
he applied to Fénelon, asking him to send him some
extracts from the chief mystical writers.

Some of the things of which he read in Mme
Guyon's writings must have startled him. The inner
voices, Grace so abounding within her as to split her
corsets, her prophecies and miracles, the dream in
which she dreamt herself the equal of the Mother of
God, or the passage in which she claimed to be the
pregnant woman of the Apocalypse, destined to
become the mother of millions of spiritual children
and to bring about the victory of the martyrs of the
Holy Ghost—all this must have astonished him not
a little ; but what most engaged his attention was
her self-avowed inability to ask, in prayer, for anything in her own behalf, her complete resignation to

God's will, whether it involved her salvation or damnation. All this looked perilously like fatalism or that terrible doctrine of predestination preached by Calvin and his followers. 'Why cannot you pray to the Saints or to the Virgin any more?' he asked her when he saw her face to face a little later on. 'Because' she made reply, 'it is not fitting for the Bride, but rather for the servants, to pray others to pray for them.' Then he questioned her regarding her prayers to God. 'I pointed out to her in her writings,' he says, 'and I made her confirm it, that every request made in one's own behalf is selfish, and contrary to pure love. She said that she could ask nothing for herself.' Then Bossuet questioned her about the Lord's prayer; could she say that? Could she ask that her sins might be forgiven? And she answered, no. Then said Bossuet: 'I command you, or rather God through me commands you, to say after me "God, I pray Thee, forgive me my trespasses." Whereto she answered: "I can repeat the words quite easily, but to get the feeling of them into my heart is contrary to my way of praying."'

The day after that cross-examination, Bossuet saw her again, at Fénelon's. He thought it would suffice for him to point out to the Abbé certain glaring passages in his friend's books, to convince him that she was in error, and suffering from delusions.

But no. Fénelon argued that it was one thing to condemn the doctrine, another to condemn the woman. Mme Guyon was in many respects ignorant; she was at any rate no theologian; therefore there was nothing to be surprised at if she expressed herself in language that was not theologically exact. Fénelon vehemently defended Mme Guyon; he believed in her dreams, her prophecies, her miracles, or was at least disposed to believe in them. He would agree to no swift and sweeping condemnation.

BOSSUET

This was too much for the burly, Burgundian commonsense of Bossuet. ' I went away,' he says, ' amazed to see so distinguished a mind lost in admiration of a woman whose vision was so limited, whose merit was so slight and whose illusions were so obvious ; a woman who was clearly posing as a prophetess.'

And that, to the average observer, would be a pretty accurate summing up of Mme Guyon. Bossuet, as we have already said, was, for all the splendours of his rhetoric, a monument of commonsense, he was the spokesman—and how eloquent a spokesman !—of the bourgeois conscience, and that is how, quite honestly, he judged this woman. And it must be confessed there was a deal to be said for the verdict. She was extravagant, often incoherent and self-contradictory in her writings and, still more, in her utterances. She wrote, by the way, at a tremendous rate, in bed at night, giving free rein to her thoughts, writing down whatever came into her head, never pausing to reflect or consider. Often she would write in a single night what it took an amanuensis four days to transcribe. Yet, in not a little of her writing, there is charm and colour and warmth and high spirituality. Thus there was, beyond the things which Bossuet observed, a hint of something, a *je ne sais quoi*, which escaped even so powerful and penetrating a glance as that of the Eagle of Meaux. But in the eyes of Fénelon that *je ne sais quoi* was so clear and so wonderful that, in the face of every obstacle, in the face of the King's displeasure, and to the ruin of his own material prospects, he refused to be a party to the condemnation of Mme Guyon. If, as was averred, certain heterodox and quite impossible ideas were implicit in her writings, they were, the Abbé de Fénelon knew, not implicit in her heart.

Mme Guyon, nevertheless, bowed her head to the

verdict. But while she indicated her submission in language of becoming deference, she sought, it seems at Fénelon's instigation, to have her case examined again, and before a wider court. For this, Bossuet, with a largeness of heart that does him credit, and contrasts strangely with the narrow vindictiveness he displayed later on when the conflict, interminably protracted, grew more embittered, bore her no malice ; he even offered to assist. The Dukes of Beauvilliers and Chevreuse signified their willingness to lend their good offices. Application was accordingly made to M. de Noailles, who was then Bishop of Châlons and who, the following year, succeeded de Harlay as Archbishop of Paris, and to M. Tronson, who had formerly been Fénelon's spiritual director at Saint-Sulpice. Noailles had been a fellow-pupil with Fénelon at the Collège du Plessis when the latter came up from Cahors to continue his studies in Paris under the tutelage of his uncle, the Marquis de Fénelon.

But the tribunal thus constituted had a different and a wider task before it than that which had confronted Bossuet. It was not so much Mme Guyon who was now on trial, as mysticism itself. The duty in short which these three ecclesiastics laid upon themselves was to sift the false mysticism from the true. Fénelon hoped that M. Tronson and M. de Noailles would have a restraining influence on Bossuet, who had, it was evident, little knowledge of, and less sympathy with, Mysticism. His God was transcendent, not immanent.

Issy, the 'country house' of Saint-Sulpice, was chosen as the scene of the deliberation of these learned men, out of regard for M. Tronson, whose age and infirmities made it difficult for him to travel farther afield. Issy was then pretty much as Renan knew it several generations later, and as, in his *Souvenirs d'Enfance et de Jeunesse*, he tenderly portrays it.

' The building,' he says, ' is situated at the
far end of an immense park and possesses no
features of any particular interest save a central
pavilion which engages the attention of the
spectator by reason of the elegance and delicacy
of its architecture. This pavilion had been the
summer residence of Marguerite de Valois,
Henri IV's first wife, and she lived there from
1606 until her death in 1615. . . . Here, in
this pavilion, she gathered round her all the
choicest spirits of the age, and Michel Bouteroue's *Petit Olympe d'Issy* is a picture of this
court, in which neither gaiety nor wit was
lacking.'

Bouteroue could turn a pretty rhyme, in the elegant
and artificial manner of his day. ' Je veux,' he sings,

Je veux d'un excellent ouvrage
Dedans un portrait racourcy,
Représenter le païsage
Du petit Olympe d'Issy,
Pourveu que la grande princesse,
La perle et fleur de l'univers,
A qui cet ouvrage s'adresse
Veuille favoriser mes vers.

Qu'on ne vante plus la Touraine
Pour son air doux et gracieux,
Ny Chenonceaus, qui d'une reyne
Fut le jardin délicieux,
Ny le Tivoly magnifique
Où, d'un artifice nouveau,
Se faict une douce musique
Des accords du vent et de l'eau.

Issy de beauté les surpasse
En beaux jardins et prés herbus,
Dignes d'estre au lieu de Parnasse
Le séjour des sœurs de Phébus.
Mainte belle source ondoyante,
Découlant de cent lieux divers,
Maintient sa terre verdoyante
Et ses arbrisseaux toujours verds.

' After Queen Margot's death, the house was sold and became the property of several successive Parisian families who lived on there until about 1655. Olier (the founder of Saint-Sulpice) occupied it during the concluding years of his life and thus turned to religious uses a habitation which had hitherto seemed little likely to have so pious a destiny. M. de Bretonvilliers, his successor, gave it to Saint-Sulpice and made it a branch of the Paris establishment. No changes were made in the little pavilion as the Queen had known it. Extensive wings were added, and a few modifying touches given to the paintings. . . . The emblems with their Spanish devices that filled the vacant spaces gave offence to no one. The park, so melodiously celebrated by Bouteroue, has been kept exactly as it was. Two or three little shrines and some statues of a religious character are the only additions. A summer-house, decorated with an inscription and two busts, is the place where Bossuet and Fénelon, M. Tronson and M. de Noailles had long conferences together on the subject of Quietism and came to an agreement which was embodied in the thirty-four articles of the spiritual life, commonly called " the Articles of Issy." . . . Ah, me ! that lovely, mystical park of Issy ! '

' Long conferences,' indeed ! They began in mid-July 1694, and if some of them were held in ' the little summer-house,' it is certain that all were not, for they continued until February or March of the following year.

While the commission was sitting, and while true mysticism was being diligently sifted from the false, the Archbishop of Paris, M. de Harlay, got wind of the proceedings, and swiftly decided on a course of

action. Whatever the verdict of the commission
of inquiry at Issy, he, de Harlay, made up his mind
to one thing, and that was that Mme Guyon should
have short shrift at his hands. He therefore hurled
his bolt with great promptitude and, on October 16,
1694, formally condemned the *Moyen Court* and
the *Cantique des Cantiques* of Mme Guyon, together
with Père La Combe's *Analyse de l'Oraison mentale.*
De Harlay had already had Mme Guyon put into
prison once. It was by no means unlikely that he
would do so again. Daunted at the prospect, and
not knowing whither to turn for refuge in her peril,
or supposed peril, she, strangely enough, asked
Bossuet to protect her. Such a request is a tribute
to his honesty, to the integrity of his character. An
indifferent mystic he may have been, but he was
unquestionably *un brave homme.* He was an
adversary, but he was an honourable one. Bossuet
invited her to take up her quarters in the Convent of
the Visitation at Meaux. It was now the depth of
winter. The Duchesse de Mortemart took her
thither in her coach, and there she arrived on
January 13, 1695.

Whatever the attitude of the Commissioners
towards Mme Guyon, they were all three anxious
to deal tactfully and tenderly with Fénelon. We
have seen how in his seminary days the latter deemed
himself in perfect spiritual communion with Tronson,
Tronson who, when his sometime pupil was chosen
as tutor to the Duc de Bourgogne, warned him
against that form of vainglory which is all the more
insidious when it comes masquerading as humility,
warned him against the risk we all run of deluding
ourselves with the idea that an honour is unsought
because we have never solicited it in set terms, or in
a definite petition. Bossuet, too, had loved Fénelon,
the brilliant pupil who had always been so friendly
and so docile, the pupil who, even now, on the

eve of these Issy discussions, had written to his one-
time guide and protector protesting his readiness
to defer to him in terms of almost exaggerated affection. ' Do not be troubled about me,' he had said,
' I am as a little child in your hands. I can assure
you that my doctrine is not my doctrine ; it simply
passes through me without leaving anything behind
it. I insist on nothing, and the whole matter is as
it were foreign, extraneous to me. I am as willing
to believe in one fashion as in another. As soon
as you have spoken, I shall make a clean sweep of the
whole thing.'

These are protestations which Bossuet must have
found a little embarrassing, and, judged in the light
of what came after, more than a little hard to explain.
M. de Noailles, than whom no one was less ' intran-
sigeant,' was an old school-friend who had sat under
the same ferule as Fénelon at the Collège du Plessis.
Their concern was far less with Mme Guyon than
with Fénelon whom, in their opinion, she had most
unaccountably perverted and misled. The great
thing in their view was to restore their friend to his
right mind, to call him back to the beaten, traditional
path—the only safe one—and, incidentally, to a
sense of his own interests. That done, Mme Guyon,
with her dreams, and her prophecies, and her
vapouring, could fly away into space, or withdraw
again into that obscurity from which she ought
never to have emerged. With a delicacy and a
bonne volonté that did honour to their hearts and
their ingenuity they conceived a way of bringing him
back to the path of orthodoxy without putting him
to the humiliation of making anything in the shape
of a retractation.

They decided to ask him to sign the articles with
them, for all the world as if he himself had taken part
in their deliberations and in the framing of their
conclusions. On March 18, 1695, Fénelon signed

the Articles of Issy, to which two had been added at his instigation. Six weeks before, on February 4, he had been appointed Archbishop of Cambrai. Saint-Simon, with his customary cynicism, says that, while it is true that Fénelon did not openly solicit this promotion, it was only because he hoped for a greater one, namely the Archbishopric of Paris.

Fénelon, on being informed by the King of his intention to appoint him to Cambrai, said he could hardly congratulate himself on being called to an office that would remove him from Paris and so involve the resignation of his position as preceptor to the young Princes. To which the King answered that it was his full intention that he should continue to teach the Princes, and that he should be exempted from residence in his diocese. On Fénelon's replying that such an arrangement would be an infringement of Canon Law, not to mention the dictates of his own conscience, the King waved aside this objection also, remarking that the Canons only required nine months residence in the diocese, not the full twelve. Fénelon would therefore spend three months of each year at Versailles. For the remaining nine he would continue to direct the Princes' education from Cambrai.

Next, Fénelon said that if he accepted the Archbishopric of Cambrai, he must needs resign the Abbey of St. Valery, the revenues of Cambrai being too great to allow him, in conscience, to retain any other preferment with it. This decision of Fénelon's caused great alarm among the 'pluralists,' in whom the times abounded. 'Rumour has it that you're resigning your benefice,' said the Archbishop of Rheims to Fénelon, 'what a piece of madness!' 'If so,' said Fénelon, 'the thing's done.' 'You'll ruin us all!' rejoined the other. 'What do you suppose the King is going to think of M. de Meaux, who has got several abbeys; of M. de Rheims who

I

is on the look out for more, and of all those prelates who look on a bishopric merely as a means of collecting abbeys ? What about all those who keep on asking for more, and will never be satisfied ? ' ' I condemn no one,' answered Fénelon. ' You mean,' retorted the Archbishop of Rheims, ' that every man should do as his conscience bids him ; well, my conscience tells me to keep my abbeys.'

' M. de Meaux and M. de Chartres,' says de la Baumelle, ' vied with each other for the honour of performing Fénelon's consecration, the latter adducing his rights as diocesan, the former relying on the claims of friendship. At Fénelon's urgent request, de Marais gave way to Bossuet, but resolved that since he was not to perform the ceremony, he would not be a witness.' The Bishop of Chartres having thus retired, his place as second assistant was taken by the Bishop of Amiens, the Bishop of Châlons being the first assistant, and Bossuet the chief consecrator.

The ceremony of consecration took place in the chapel of St. Cyr on June 10, 1695, in the presence of a gathering which included Mme de Maintenon and Fénelon's royal pupils. After his consecration, the new Archbishop at once proceeded to his diocese.

' The honour which the King has bestowed on me,' he said, in a letter to a friend, ' is one of the highest one can receive at the hands of any man ; but all that man can give is but " vanity and vexation of spirit " as the Preacher hath it. We can but look on this as a heavy burden and endeavour faithfully to sustain it. It is with me now, as it was with St. Peter. " When thou wert young," said our Lord to him, " thou wentest whither thou wouldest ; but when thou shalt be old, another shall gird thee, and

carry thee whither thou wouldest not." I have had
a happy, free youth filled with agreeable study and
intercourse with delightful friends. Now I go forth
to enter upon a perpetual servitude in a strange land.
Sometimes I am sensible of the change ; but it were
an ill thing for me to cling too inordinately to health,
or freedom, or friends, or any other solace.'

'Two days before the consecration,' Bossuet has
put on record, 'falling on his knees and kissing the
hand that was to consecrate him, he took it to witness
that he had never professed any different doctrine
from mine. In my heart, if I may so express it,
it was I who was kneeling to him, rather than he to
me. . . . M. de Châlons was begged to be one of
the assistants at the consecration, and we both
believed we were giving to the Church a prelate
whose convictions would ever be unanimous with
his consecrators'.'

But it was then, when all seemed happily composed—for during the Issy conferences Fénelon
never ceased to profess his absolute obedience—
that the rift appeared, and began rapidly to widen.
Bossuet, by way of epitomising the whole business,
composed a sort of epilogue, setting his seal as it
were on the findings of the Commission. He called
it *Instructions sur les États d'Oraison.*

Meantime Mme Guyon, growing weary of her
long captivity, for such in effect it was, made application through Bossuet to the King for leave to go and
drink the waters at Bourbon-les-Eaux. And then,
without waiting for a reply, she made her escape,
with the connivance and complicity of the Duchesse
de Mortemart. She took refuge in a little house in
the Faubourg Saint-Antoine. There she was discovered and was immediately hurried off to Vincennes.
Nine months later she was put into a convent at
Vaugirard. Finally, after continual failures to keep
her promises, she was shut up in the Bastille.

Unfortunately Bossuet was not content to deal with ideas alone. He must needs fulminate against ' the person who composed the book entitled *Moyen Court.*'

Before his book was published, Bossuet sent proofs to Fénelon, Tronson and Noailles for their endorsement. Fénelon kept the proofs one night only, and sent them back to their author *unapproved.* He was not going to forsake Mme Guyon. Rather than leave her in the lurch, he would sacrifice his whole career, and live in perpetual exile. ' Un prodige de séduction ! ' exclaimed Bossuet, and the voice of commonsense was overwhelmingly on his side. But was the voice of commonsense so wholly in the right ? The voice of commonsense before now, has been uncommonly unjust. Was this such an instance ?

Meanwhile Fénelon sits down to write his *Maximes des Saints* at which he toils with all the energy at his command. It was printed off with the utmost celerity and, before the *États d'Oraison*, it was given to the public. Thus was kindled one of the mightiest, and one of the bitterest controversies in the whole history of religion ; and these two men, each of them a genius in his own way, and once such loyal friends, became the fiercest and most implacable of foes.

CHAPTER XI

THE WORD AND THE SPIRIT

IT is something of a paradox that a book written by one of the most graceful of writers at a moment when it behoved him to state his case with all the persuasiveness at his command, should, in the event, have proved to be the most arid production that ever came from his pen. The plan of the *Explication des Maximes des Saints* is mechanical in its rigidity. It consists of ninety articles, forty-five setting forth the true mysticism, forty-five the false, arranged alternately, first a true, then a false, and so on.

Two days after the book appeared, Bossuet wrote to his nephew the Abbé saying : ' It is a fact that M. de Cambrai has refused to approve my book on the grounds that he will not incriminate Mme Guyon. A couple of days ago, he brought out a book of his own on spiritual matters the whole object of which is to bolster up her case, though he never mentions her by name.'

The *Maximes des Saints* had a very indifferent reception. Bossuet saw to it that the King should be under no misapprehension as to its pernicious nature, remarking at the same time that the whole thing was so subtle and wire-drawn from beginning to end that ordinary people wouldn't understand a word of it. Bossuet's own book, *Instructions sur les États d'Oraison*, which came out a month later, scored a resounding success.

And now the great controversy—one of the most

memorable in the Church's history—began. Bossuet beat to arms. He had once loved Fénelon ; Fénelon his tender, docile *alumnus*, so engaging, so full of promise, had been the apple of his eye. And now all that sweetness turned to gall. Henceforth, it was to be war between them, war *à outrance*, and all the crueller for the love that had once united them. To Bossuet's robust, practical mind, Fénelon's attitude was stark, unmitigated folly, mingled with a sort of petulant perversity that robbed him of all his patience. To Bossuet, as to the King, Mme Guyon was, if not completely demented, fundamentally unbalanced and deranged. Her doctrine, if one could dignify her incoherent ravings with such a name, was certainly (he deemed) infected with the taint of Molinism, than which nothing more pernicious, nothing more abominable could be conceived. It was the strangest thing in the world that Fénelon, with all his gifts of mind and spirit, all his exalted religious fervour, should have suffered himself to be so fatally misled. Yet, every consideration had been shown him. He had not been asked to retract ; no formal recantation had ever been demanded of him. The whole matter had been managed with the most studied regard for his feelings and his *amour-propre*. He had been invited to sign the articles of Issy as if he had borne a part in framing them. He had been made to appear, not a defendant but a judge. And now when he—Bossuet—composed for popular consumption a book summarising and commenting on the whole affair, Fénelon withheld his approval, because, forsooth, the book struck at Mme Guyon.

We may here pause to consider what this Molinism was of which Bossuet was so genuinely afraid and with which he believed Mme Guyon and Fénelon himself to be tainted. Molinos was originally a priest at Saragossa who, in 1670, quitted that city

and went to Rome, where he became the director of
a number of people, many of them belonging to the
noblest families.   Five years after his arrival in
Rome, he published in his own tongue a manual of
devotion which he called *The Spiritual Guide.*   The
book was an immediate success and was forthwith
translated into French, Latin, Dutch, and German.
It was not until six years after the publication of his
book (and eleven after his arrival in Rome) that an
Italian Jesuit named Signori drew attention to its
alleged errors.   A commission was appointed to
examine the book.   It reported nothing contrary
to Christian doctrine.   The Jesuits returned to the
charge.   The book had attained a wide vogue in
France.   Père La Chaise prevailed on Louis XIV to
intervene.   On his representations, Molinos was
arrested and brought before the Roman Inquisition.
After a protracted enquiry, Molinos was condemned
to withdraw sixty-eight points which were either
contained in his writings, or were deducible from
them.   And so, arrayed in sackcloth, the once
fashionable director made his humble retractation
in the presence of the full Roman court and as many
of the public as contrived to gain admittance.   Now
this, in brief, is the doctrine of Molinos as set forth
in his Spiritual Guide :

Perfection is attainable even in this life.   It
consists in one continuous, uninterrupted act of
contemplation and love.   The state, when attained,
is indefectible.   It continues even during sleep.
No reiteration or renewal of the act is needed by
those who have once attained to the state of perfect
contemplation.

In this state, in which the soul is merged entirely
in God, it is occupied with no separate or distinct
object of thought.   Its own faculties become as
nothing ;   it abandons itself wholly to God.   The
soul thinks no more of reward or punishment.   It

thinks neither of Heaven nor Hell ; neither of Death nor Eternity. All desire of sanctification is put aside, and even to its own salvation the soul is indifferent.

In this state of perfect contemplation, confession, mortification, good works are useless, and even harmful, as tending to interrupt it.

Perfect prayer requires entire obliviousness of every distinct thought, of the attributes of God, or of the Trinity, or of the mysteries of Jesus Christ. He who in his praying bethinks himself of any distinct idea or object, of any concept of his mind, does not worship God in spirit and in truth.

Once we have resigned our will to God, we need have no more heed of the temptations that assail us, nor need we attempt to resist them. These things do but affect our lower nature, the higher is beyond their reach. Man is no longer accountable to God even for his most sinful acts. His body may become the instrument of the Devil, but in such transactions, the soul, unconcerned with what passes in its carnal dwelling, has no part.

These grievous trials of the flesh are a short and certain way to purge and extinguish the passions. The soul which has passed through this purgation is no longer conscious of rebellion, and commits no further sin, not even a venial one.

The penultimate paragraph, which declares the soul to have no responsibility for what goes on in the body, was held to constitute a danger and a scandal, and with good reason. Evidently the Church had no choice but to combat with all her energy a teaching that would reduce the will of man to complete impotence, render him indifferent to his own salvation, and invite him, not only to offer no resistance to temptation, but even to encourage the sins of the flesh in order that they might be conquered by satiety. Of this pernicious doctrine, Mme Guyon's teaching, though it stresses the continued act of contemplation and love, as merging within it all separate religious acts, shows no trace. Fénelon, in the *Maximes des Saints*, expressly condemns the alleged indefectibility of those who, by some initial and supposedly all-sufficing act, have put themselves into communion with God. He makes perfection consist in an habitual state of simple love, in which the hope of reward and the fear of punishment have ceased to play a part. But let it be granted for the sake of argument that Mme Guyon's doctrine did contain within it the germ of Molinism. Even so, it is one thing to condemn the doctrine, but quite another to impeach and imprison the teacher. There is, Fénelon held, no moral justification for that, provided that she erred in good faith and that her intentions were pure.

Up to now the commonsense of the matter seems to have rested with Bossuet. Here was a woman, an obvious *détraquée*, who had been preaching doctrines which, so far as they were intelligible at all, were undoubtedly heretical. The case had been judged, the Articles of Issy had been drawn up in order that the truth about mysticism might be fully and clearly brought out; Fénelon himself had signed these Articles. Why then did he obstinately refuse to approve of a book which was merely a restatement of these Articles? The answer was that the book condemned Mme Guyon. Was it then really worth while to quarrel about a person of such small importance?

Let us now hear what Fénelon had to say about Mme Guyon, and about the regard in which he held her, a regard which, if Bossuet's estimate of her mental powers and character were a true one, would indeed be hard to explain.

' I became acquainted with Mme Guyon,' writes Fénelon, ' early in the year 1689, some time after she had left the Convent of the Visitation in the rue

Saint-Antoine, and a few months before I went to court. At that time I was not very favourably disposed towards her on account of what I had heard of her holding-forth and missionizing up and down the country. What tended very considerably to modify the unflattering opinion I entertained about her was a letter dated June 29, 1683, from the late Bishop of Geneva, which contains the following reference to the lady in question :

' " I have the greatest esteem for her and regard her as very superior to Père La Combe. But I cannot approve of her eagerness to impress her ideas on everybody and to introduce them into all our convents and monasteries to the prejudice of the ideals of their founders. That is productive of quarrels and divisions even in the saintliest communities. That is the only grievance I have against her. Apart from that, I esteem and honour her more than I can say." On reading those words, I saw that all the Bishop complained of was the intemperate zeal of a woman who was over-anxious to share with others the good thing she thought she had found. Save for that, he esteemed her beyond expression. Although in 1688 this Bishop put a ban on Mme Guyon's books, he was still holding her in the highest regard as late as February 8, 1695, for on that date he wrote as follows : " I have never heard her spoken of save with the greatest esteem and respect, and neither my memory nor my conscience reproaches me with ever having spoken of her otherwise. Little drawn as I may have been to her Quietist ideas and to the works of Père La Combe, I have never had anything but praise for her piety and moral conduct."

' Now the Bishop of Meaux will very likely say that the testimony of the late Bishop of Geneva proves nothing, seeing that he had never read the *Life* of Mme Guyon, or any other of her fanatical writings. Well, if that is so, let me quote another witness, a witness who has read and studied Mme Guyon's manuscripts, every one of them, from beginning to end. M. de Meaux ought not to have any objection to this witness, for he is—none other than M. de Meaux himself! He kept her for six months in the Convent of the Visitandines at Meaux because he thought she had bemused me. He then read, not only all her printed books, but all her manuscripts—all those writings in which he now assures us she exposes her absolute fanaticism. Surely, then, he, if anybody, might be expected to mistrust her. If I had been misled, there would have been no excuse whatever for his following my example. The fact that I, to his great astonishment, had been led astray, ought to have been a sufficient safeguard against his falling into the same trap. Nevertheless, this is how he treated her while she was in his diocese : he admitted her to the sacraments from the first, and continued to do so, never calling on her to acknowledge or retract any error whatsoever. Subsequently, after reading all her manuscripts and carefully examining the lady herself, he dictated to her a form of submission in which, after repudiating and condemning all the errors imputed to her, she was to add the following : " I nevertheless declare with all respect, and without prejudice to the present declaration and act of submission, that I never wilfully intended to advance any opinion that might be contrary to the spirit of the Catholic, Apostolic, and Roman Church, to which I always have submitted, and to which, God willing, I always shall submit until my dying breath." By this document, which M. de Meaux has not seen fit to quote, he himself endorses the intentions of the lady, for what she wrote she wrote at his dictation. Nor is that all. M. de Meaux dictated to her the following statement which was

to be appended to the " charge " in which he had
censured her works : " I never entertained any of
the errors set forth in the accompanying Pastoral
Letter, for it was ever my wish and intention to write
in a perfectly Catholic sense, nor did I realise at the
time that any other sense could be put upon my
words. I am grieved beyond measure to think that
my ignorance and my lack of familiarity with
theological terminology should have exposed me to
condemnation." This is what M. de Meaux, after
reading all her manuscripts, dictated to Mme Guyon
in order that, in justice to herself, she might explain
her intentions, explain, that is to say, the sense in
which she herself understood her works when she
wrote them.'

It will be seen that, all along, Fénelon's concern is
not so much with what she had said, not so much with
the interpretation which a strict theologian might
put upon her words—not that, but rather with what
she *intended*, with what she really had in her heart.
Bossuet further declared that he had pointed out to
Fénelon in Mme Guyon's books all the errors and
exaggerations of which she had been guilty. ' What,'
asks Fénelon, ' does he mean by that ? ' ' Does he
mean that he brought the books to me and actually
pointed out these things, then and there ? That is
apparently what he wishes people to infer, though he
does not say so in so many words. He boasts of his
memory, but his memory does not allow him to speak
unequivocally on this point. The real truth is that
in the course of a somewhat brief conversation,
which he calls a " conference," he told me about
her " visions." And what did I reply ? In the first
place, I declared that she must be mad and impious
if she had really spoken of herself in such a way. I
then remarked that many saintly people had in all
good faith told of certain particular graces they had
received from God, but nothing of the extravagant

nature here in question.   Next, I did say that this lady had seemed to me rather inclined to exaggerate her experiences.   Lastly, I referred to the words of St. Paul which M. de Meaux had himself taken as his rule : " Prove ye men's minds, whether they be of God."

' The things which M. de Meaux told me were new to me and well nigh incredible.   I began, I confess, to wonder whether M. de Meaux had not been rather carried away by his prejudices against this lady.   I quite failed to recognize in any of the things he told me anything resembling the sentiments I had always thought I discerned in Mme Guyon. It seemed to me that she must either be a lunatic or an impostor if she desired people to believe that she herself took seriously and literally all the things I was hearing about her.   It is naturally disagreeable to be called upon to believe such monstrous things about one whom you have always looked upon as sensible and sincere.   Mme Guyon had frequently told me that from time to time impressions had flashed through her mind which for the moment seemed like special intimations from God, but which vanished like a fleeting dream, leaving no trace behind them. She used to add that she did not know whether these visitations were imaginary, illusory, or true ; that she did not attach great importance to them.   Far from showing any desire to question her in detail about these things, I thought it wisest to let them drop, and not to appear to assign any serious weight to them.

' In coming to this conclusion, I was following no hasty ideas of my own.   It was the rule followed by Blessed John of the Cross, by Teresa of Avila and by many others of the most renowned mystics in the Church, among them Père Surin of whom M. de Meaux himself approves.   That writer observes that very saintly people may be deceived by the cunning

of Satan, as St. Catherine was for three years by the
Devil in the guise of Jesus Christ and the Holy
Virgin. According to him, the way for people
suffering under these illusions to prevent themselves
from going astray, is to cling firmly to the Faith and
to the rule of obedience. It was these considerations
that led me to hope that M. de Meaux would,
according to the rule of St. Paul, make trial of Mme
Guyon " to see whether she was of God." I added
that I thought she might be deceived, but not that
she was a deceiver.'

Later, Fénelon says : ' The reader must not be
surprised that I furnished M. de Meaux with
memoranda regarding the mystical life, for it was he
who asked me for them. It must be borne in mind
that when he was brought into this enquiry he had
never read St. Francis de Sales, or any other of the
mystics, such as Ruysbroeck, Harphius, Tauler, etc.,
of whom he says that, being unable to make anything
out of their extravagant utterances, people preferred
to let them remain unread among the lumber of the
libraries. These were the authors with whom I
deemed he ought to make himself acquainted before
passing judgement on the mystics.'

In April, 1697, Fénelon submitted his book to the
Pope, accompanying it with a letter praying him to
pass judgement upon it. Soon after that, the Pope
received another letter bearing on the matter, this
time from the King. It informed him that the book
had been examined in France by a committee of
prelates and theologians who had pronounced it
' evil and dangerous.' That letter was dated July 26.
On August 1 Fénelon was commanded by the King
to withdraw to his diocese. On the following day,
Fénelon quitted Versailles, never to return.
Fénelon's colleagues, de Langeron and de Beaumont,
who had assisted him in his tutorial duties were also
dismissed and went with him into exile.

Meanwhile Bossuet pursued the campaign with relentless energy. The great duel went on ; Bossuet, with the King and most of the French clergy behind him ; Fénelon deserted and alone. The great duel went on, attack and reply, retort and rejoinder, charge and counter-charge following each other in quick and seemingly endless succession. It would be useless to attempt to enter into the details of the long conflict, to follow phase after phase of this great war of words. Each of the combatants believed that he was in the right. Each was acting in perfect good faith. Bossuet was convinced that he was fighting a very grave peril to the Church ; Fénelon was no less certain that his mysticism was no more unorthodox than the mysticism of St. John of the Cross or St. Francis de Sales.

And all this bitterness, all this tremendous output of energy, what a strange and—one cannot help exclaiming—what an unedifying spectacle ! And, on one side at least, all this wire-pulling, all this rather ignoble intrigue—*Tantæne animis cœlestibus*— ! And what if, after all, the whole unhappy quarrel were due to a misunderstanding. Someone is said to have drawn up a formula, a statement of mystical doctrine and shown it first to one and then to the other of the disputants. And both of them agreed to it ! Was it some little fault of temper, some tiny speck of dust which had started an irritation that had grown and grown till it was past curing and past endurance ? Both were men of genius, both were men of the loftiest character, both aspired to walk with God and do His will. Nevertheless, if one exhibited a little petulance, a little suspicion of something one hardly dares to call obstinacy, the other may have been a little over-anxious about his position, his preponderance, his grandeur. At any rate the quarrel became a personal one, or largely so. Pride, or at least *amour-propre*, played no small part, one suspects, in this unending feud. Unending indeed, for they never bridged the gulf between them. Neither time, which heals most wounds, nor distance, availed to remove the sense of bitterness and wrong which each harboured in his heart. Death came and found them still unreconciled.

CHAPTER XII

ROMA LOCUTA EST

IN Rome, Bossuet's nephew, the Abbé, was indefatigable on his uncle's behalf. The Eagle of Meaux was hardly to be congratulated on his agent. He was certainly energetic, he was quite untroubled by scruples, he detested Fénelon and his motto was ' Victory at any price, no matter what the means.' He was ' loud,' vulgar, and his establishment was ostentatious, far more notable for its magnificence than its taste. The theologians were busy on the incriminated book, examining it microscopically, sentence by sentence. It would be well, thought the Abbé, to create an atmosphere prejudicial to its author, a task to which he devoted himself with a will. Père La Combe, dragged about from prison to prison, had died raving mad at Charenton. But before his senses had completely deserted him, a sort of confession had been wrung from him. He avowed that error and sinfulness had attended some of his relations with Mme Guyon, that there had in fact been over-much freedom between them. Mme Guyon, confronted with this confession, said (in a letter to Mme de Beauvilliers) : ' It is true that when Père La Combe came back after months of absence in the country he used to embrace me, taking my head in his hands. He did this quite simply and naturally, and I was just as natural with him.' The Abbé took care to have all this disseminated in Rome, and with it a letter which Fénelon had written to Mme de Maintenon in 1697,

in which he actually called Mme Guyon, *mon amie !*
' Let those who only know her by her writings,'
Fénelon had said, ' judge those writings strictly
according to the letter. For me it is different. I
know what was in her mind, and it is only right that
I should interpret her writings accordingly ; not
that I should judge her thoughts by the rigorously
literal sense of her writings.' ' She is an unhappy
creature,' he adds, ' caught in the toils, bowed down
with sorrow and abuse, with none to defend her,
none to take her part.'

As Saint-Simon observes, Fénelon was not only the
prelate, he was very emphatically the *grand seigneur*.
He would have sacrificed his life, let alone his career,
rather than abandon the woman whom he had
befriended, and to whom he deemed himself
spiritually indebted, to the woman who was, in the
highest and the truest sense, his *friend*.

Meantime, while the Abbé Bossuet was busy
poisoning the air, M. de Meaux was no less busy
with his pen. In June, 1697, his *Relation sur le
Quiétisme* came out and caused a tremendous
sensation. Bossuet was a master of irony and here
he had employed his gift to the full. People were
amused, delighted—they could talk of nothing
else. It was another proof, if such were needed,
that he was the prince of pamphleteers, that his
talents had not even begun to fail him. Bossuet was
well pleased with his handiwork. ' *Ah, oui, je suis
en bon train !* ' he exclaimed with glee. Bossuet's
partisans were jubilant, Fénelon's proportionately
dismayed. Fénelon himself was unmoved. He sent
a copy of the *Relation* to de Chanterac who was
watching over his interests in Rome, with a few
marginal notes which, he said, were answer enough
to his opponent's allegations. De Chanterac
urged that this was not enough, that the answer must
be as public as the charge. Fénelon was persuaded,

MME DE MAINTENON

and addressed himself with such energy to the task that on August 2 he announced that he had finished his reply ; by the 30th, a copy of the work reached Rome. Once more the tables were turned. The *Réponse à la Relation* was as great a triumph as the *Relation* had been. People did not know what to admire most in it, its clearness, its accuracy, its logical and orderly arrangement, the simplicity, the elegance, the nobility of its style. But what was most important, most impressive, was that it bore upon it the unmistakable hall-mark of truth. ' If M. de Meaux has any further document or testimony to bring forward against me, I beg him to make no half-secret of it, for half-secrets are more damaging than open statements. I have no fear of anything so long as it is brought out into the light of day. It is only hints and innuendoes, uninvestigated allegations that can make me uneasy. If he would defame me, let him do so openly and before my judges. For myself, I call to witness Him whose Eyes pierce the thickest darkness and before whom we must all ere long appear, that I cleave to no person and to no book, that I am bound solely to Him and His Church, beseeching Him to bring back peace, and put an end to these scandals. I entreat Him to restore His shepherds to their flocks, to gather them into His Fold, and to grant to M. de Meaux blessings as many as the trials he has heaped upon me.'

' I hope you will approve of my answer,' wrote Fénelon to de Chanterac. ' If the tone strikes you as rather stronger than usual, that is because I thought people might take my moderation for fear. At all events the tone is mildness itself, compared with that of my opponent. My health remains satisfactory, thank God, in spite of labours which might overwhelm a stronger man.'

At last, after nearly two years of deliberation, the verdict was pronounced : the *Maximes des Saints* was condemned. The news was brought to Fénelon on the Feast of the Annunciation, just as he was about to preach in the Cathedral. The blow must have been a heavy one, but he bore it with complete calmness. He may have felt a sensation of relief that the long period of suspense was over at last. At once he changed the subject of his discourse and, instead of dwelling on the significance of the festival they were keeping, he preached, to an audience, often moved to tears, on the duty, the sacred duty, of submitting to the rulers of the Church. Fénelon bowed to the decree without repining, without a murmur. The voice of the Church was the voice of God. And the Church had spoken. Nevertheless, he knew in his heart that his doctrine was sound. If he had erred, he had erred, not in the substance of his thought, but in the expression of it. ' I never *thought* the errors imputed to me. It is quite easy for me, as a mark of obedience to the Pope, to condemn my book as expressing what I never thought I was expressing ; but I cannot do my conscience the wrong of cravenly accepting blame for errors that I never dreamt of committing. . . . The Pope understands my book better than I understand it myself. And to that I submit. But as to my thoughts, as to what is in my mind, I can only say that that is a matter on which I speak with greater authority than anyone ; it is the only subject on which, without presumption, I can claim to be better informed than any other.'

Years after, in a letter to Père Le Tellier, the King's confessor, he wrote these words : ' The late Bishop of Meaux attacked my book in favour of a pernicious and untenable doctrine, the doctrine which declares that our love of God is based solely on our hope of reward. This unworthy doctrine, which degrades the love of God by making the expectation of reward its only motive, was tolerated

and allowed to triumph. *He who was in the wrong won the day ; he who was in the right was overthrown.'*
Was Fénelon, then, sincere in his submission, in his professions of humility ? How, if he was, can the words italicised in that letter be justified ? Bossuet makes a great deal of the ' arrogance ' of his opponent's submission (*M. de Cambrai continue à faire le soumis de l'air du monde le plus arrogant*), and Fénelon's opponents had all counted confidently on his rebellion. ' You will see,' said Bossuet, ' when it comes to the point, what his protestations of humility will be worth ! ' His submission they therefore found not a little disconcerting. This would account for the doubts they cast on its sincerity. Nevertheless, people have asked in all good faith whether it is possible for a man suddenly to change his beliefs at the behest of an external authority. Whether in such a case his submission is necessarily outward, not inward. Did Fénelon now conscientiously repudiate those great mystics on whose teaching he had set such store and by whom he professed to have been inspired ? Was there henceforth no room for mysticism in the Church ? This sort of question was not unnatural, and, according to Ramsay, Fénelon himself supplied the answer. He admitted that he had reproduced expressions which he had found in the books of the greater mystics ; but the authors of those books were not theologians, and it was not to be expected of them that they should define their thoughts with the rigid precision of one formally presenting a theological dogma. But exaggerations and inexactitudes which may be explained and excused when they occur in the writings of private individuals take on an entirely different aspect when they are presented for universal acceptance by one of the Church's leaders. There was nothing out of the way in Fénelon's admitting that he had given to certain phrases in the writings

of the great mystics an over liberal interpretation. He felt that he might well have laid himself open to this reproach and, so he proceeded, while the case of his book was still *sub judice*, to define with greater theological exactitude certain passages therein that might have been liable to misinterpretation. With such care had these modifications and corrections been effected that the Court which condemned the book had no criticisms to offer against the explanatory supplement. This fact and its implications are dealt with at length in Cardinal de Bausset's *Life of Fénelon ;* suffice it to say here that the Papal Brief condemned, not the doctrine of mystical prayer, which is the highest human love of God for His own sake, because He is infinitely adorable, but Fénelon's expression of that doctrine in certain parts of his *Maximes*. There are those who see in the phrase : 'He who was in the wrong won the day, he who was in the right was overthrown,' a revolt against the judgement to which he had pretended to submit. They should read on, and see what, on their hypothesis, they can make of what follows : ' I attach not the slightest value to my book, and I cheerfully sacrificed it in obedience to command.' But the doctrine itself remained. What was condemned was a certain presentation of it in a certain book. And it is to be noted that in the terms of that condemnation ' heresy' was not mentioned. It was not even hinted at.

But in judging the whole case there are certain circumstances peculiar to the times that must on no account be lost sight of. It is important to bear in mind that Molinos, with his doctrine about the non-responsibility of the soul for the sins of the body, had brought, at least for ordinary practical minds, even the highest forms of mysticism under suspicion. So prejudicial to the mystics was the atmosphere created by the Molinos scandal that if Ste. Jeanne Chantal, if St. Francis de Sales himself, had flourished and taught a decade or two later, they, too, might have come under the ban.

Now though this pernicious doctrine of Molinos was rejected by Mme Guyon, she professed ideas that tended to render nugatory the sacramental life and ritual worship of the Church. These ideas Fénelon himself had in his turn repudiated in the Articles of Issy, maintaining only that our love of God should be so pure, so absolute, as to make us regardless of reward, regardless even of our own salvation.

Bossuet, however, considered, and practical people will agree with him, that to discard salvation as an incentive to religion was to forgo that which, among the general run of men, was the most powerful of all reasons for living the religious life. If Fénelon was carried too far in stating his doctrine of the absolute love of God, Bossuet was incapable of recognising that Fénelon's doctrine had any validity at all. In spite of the length of the controversy which raged so bitterly between them, the combatants never really met on common ground. How could they ? The realms of Bossuet's mind, vast and splendid as they were, were meted and confined. Fénelon's spirit, impatient of frontiers, was ever straining after the ineffable, the inapprehensible ; striving for that infinite perfection to which no mortal may attain. He had heard a ' singing in the sails,' which was not of the breeze.

CHAPTER XIII

THE EXILE

THE Archiepiscopal Palace at Cambrai, which was destroyed by fire during the Revolution, was a noble building, imposing alike from its size and its splendour. Here the exile lived in high state, as became a *grand seigneur*, and a Prince of the Empire. In high state, yet combined with much meekness, condescending ease and graciousness on the part of the *maître du logis*. The great rooms of the palace were furnished with a kind of subdued stateliness, a monotonous and somewhat melancholy splendour. The *salle du daïs*, or state-room, was curtained and carpeted in crimson ; stiff, formal arm-chairs were ranged along the walls that were adorned with rich tapestries depicting various episodes from the Book of Genesis. Crimson, too, but fringed with gold, were the curtains that draped the doors, one at each of the four corners of the room. The high table with its canopy was on the western side of the room, facing the great carved fireplace. But nowhere, neither on chair, nor hangings, nor above the high table, nor over the fireplace, was there any blazon of armorial bearings, or any heraldic device to remind the visitor that His Grace the Archbishop belonged to one of the oldest and most illustrious families of France. With this noble apartment, the great state-bedroom was in keeping in the sombre magnificence of its furniture and trappings, which were all of crimson damask. The bed was a huge four-poster, richly caparisoned in

crimson and gold ; the walls were hung with crimson.
On the mantelpiece stood a portrait of the King of
Spain, and immediately above it a portrait of the
Grand Monarque, to the right of which hung Monseigneur the Dauphin and beyond him the Dauphin's
son—Fénelon's former pupil—Monseigneur the Duc
de Bourgogne. Besides these, there were pictures
portraying subjects taken from the Bible. Such was
the Archbishop's bedchamber ; but the Archbishop
did not sleep in it. There was a room hard by, a
room of very modest dimensions, a homely room
where the furniture was upholstered in nothing
more expensive than a sort of grey worsted, very plain
and austere, except that pictorial scenes had been
embroidered on the backs of the chairs. The bed,
it is true, was a four-poster, but it was hung with
curtains of the same hue as the rest of the furniture.
' This is my room, this is where I sleep,' His Grace
would explain to anyone he might chance to be
showing over the palace. ' The other room is for
show ; this one is for use.'

It was a lordly abode, this Palace of Cambrai, and
the scale of living was grand and stately there as
befitted so noble a master. Yet that master himself,
so far as he was personally concerned, lived with the
simplicity, the austerity of an anchorite.

For all its magnificence, an air of melancholy
brooded over the place. Fénelon was an exile, there
was no forgetting that. And what did that imply ?
To incur the royal displeasure in those days was like
catching some contagious disease. It resulted in
isolation for the sufferer. No one who sought
advancement at Court, nay, no one who merely
wanted to be let alone, to live a quiet, tranquil life,
would willingly have anything to do, save secretly,
with such a social pariah. It needed no small
measure of moral courage for anyone openly to avow
himself the exile's friend. It cannot be denied that

Fénelon felt his ostracism keenly. Great Christian
as he was, it is doubtful whether he had yet reached
those heights of renunciation to which, with the
help of the many and unceasing tribulations that
were yet in store for him, he was one day to attain.
A visit from a friend, or a kinsman, filled him with
joy, with a sober but pathetically real delight. ' I'll
have no more of you,' he writes half-playfully, half-
sadly, to a nephew who had been paying him a visit,
and from whom he had reluctantly parted, ' it is
too much of a wrench when you go.' A French
writer, M. Em. de Broglie, describing Fénelon's
latter days at Cambrai, days overshadowed by woe
upon woe, speaks of his reaching at length, along
that steep and stony calvary, to that ultimate limit
of spiritual perfection, when sorrow and disappointment have taught their final lesson, when there is
no more to learn, when death comes at last and,
gently, as with the lightest touch, gathers from its
bough the fruit that is ripe for Eternity.

As for the veneration in which Fénelon came to be
held, we have what is more convincing than the
eulogy of any friend, that is the testimony of the
Abbé Le Dieu, Bossuet's secretary, who, if any man,
must have been armed with prejudice against that
arch-adversary on whom his redoubtable master
had so long outpoured the phials of his wrath.

The Eagle of Meaux died on April 12, 1704, and
in the following September Le Dieu, actuated by no
other motive than curiosity, betook himself to
Cambrai, in order that he might see with his own
eyes and judge for himself what manner of man this
was around whom a legend was already beginning
to gather. He went, he saw, and was conquered. It
was execrable weather when the Abbé set out on his
journey ; nothing but heavy and continuous rain.
At last he arrived and took up his quarters at the
Hôtel du Lion in the great square. To his grievous

disappointment, he learned that Fénelon was absent
on a pastoral visitation in Flanders.   Disappointment, however, was swiftly turned to joy when next
morning a messenger, riding express, gave out the
news that the Archbishop was returning that day and
would arrive at the palace in time for the midday
dinner.

Le Dieu had been astute enough to arm himself
with what he felt sure would be a passport to the
Archbishop's good graces.   He had informed
Madame de Maisonfort of his intended visit, and
that lady, from whose memory the image of her
former director had never been effaced, entrusted
him with a letter to be delivered into Fénelon's own
hands.

In good time that morning, the Abbé made his
way to the palace and took up a favourable position
at the head of the grand staircase.   In due course the
Archbishop arrived, accompanied by his nephew
and chaplain the Abbé de Beaumont, and two
gentlemen from Paris who had come to pay him a
visit.   He was greeted by the Abbé de Chanterac,
his *Grand Vicaire*, supported by the principal
officers of the household, while his young nephews,
the de Fénelons, added warmth and gaiety to his
welcome.

' As soon,' says Le Dieu, ' as I saw him entering,
I respectfully drew near.   Just at first I thought his
manner a little cold, and fancied I detected the
faintest shadow of annoyance, yet he was gentle
withal, and perfectly polite.   Kindly, but without
effusion, he invited me to his room.   " I am availing
myself, Monseigneur," said I, " of Your Grace's
suggestion that I should visit you when a suitable
opportunity presented itself," adding in a lower
tone that I was the bearer of messages and a letter
from Madame de Maisonfort. . . .   The Archbishop was attired in long violet robes, cassock and

chimere, with bright crimson buttons and button-holes. There were no gold tassels or gold fringe on his girdle, and round his hat was a plain green silk cord. He was wearing white gloves, and had neither stick nor cloak. I delivered the packet I had for him as soon as we entered, and without opening it he bade me sit down in an arm-chair similar to his own. He refused to let me take a more modest seat and insisted on my wearing my hat. . . . Dinner having already been announced, he rose and invited me to a seat at his table. All the company were awaiting him in the dining-room. No one had come to his room, it being known that I was closeted with him there. We all washed our hands, one after another, without any ceremony. The Archbishop said grace and, of course, took his place at the head of the table with the Abbé de Chanterac on his left. Then, the rest of the company, when they had washed, sat down wherever it pleased them. I chose an inconspicuous seat among the others, and a plate of soup was forthwith set before me ; but the seat on the Archbishop's right being vacant, His Grace beckoned me to come and take it. I thanked him but said that I was already seated and served. With great courtesy he insisted. ' Come,' he said, ' your place is here.' After that, I obeyed his summons without further demur, and my soup was duly brought to me in my new seat.

' The table was served with tasteful magnificence. There were several kinds of soup, good beef and mutton, a variety of *entrées* and *ragoûts*, a command-ing roast, partridges, and a quanitity of other game variously dressed. The dessert was magnificent, the peaches and grapes exquisite, although we were in Flanders, and first rate pears, and various kinds of cooked or preserved fruit ; sound red wine, no beer ; spotless linen, excellent bread, and an abundance of plate, very massive and in the best style. There were a large number of servants in livery, who carried out their duties deftly, promptly and noiselessly. The Archbishop was served by a footman and sometimes by the major-domo himself. I liked the look of the latter, and he seemed to be respected and obeyed by the whole staff.

'The Archbishop was so good as to help me with his own hands to everything that was choicest on the table. Each time, as I thanked him I raised my hat, and each time, he took off his hat to me. He further did me the honour to drink my health with a grave yet easy courtesy. The conversation was similarly easy and delightful, sometimes even merry. The Archbishop took his share in the general talk and allowed everyone to have his say. I noticed that his chaplains, his secretaries and his squire joined in the conversation as freely as the rest, though no one ventured on any chaff or personal repartee. The young nephews did not talk. The Abbé de Beaumont kept the conversation going. It was mainly concerned with the Archbishop's recent journey. The Abbé was extremely well-disposed and I never noticed a trace in his manner of the arrogant and overbearing airs I have only too often encountered in other places. Indeed I met with far more modesty and meekness in master, nephews and everyone else than I had ever experienced elsewhere.'

CHAPTER XIV

THE SPIRITUAL DIRECTOR

NOWHERE is Fénelon's psychological insight, his power of analysing the human character, of penetrating into the recesses of the human soul, his ability to read the secrets of the heart, particularly, perhaps, the feminine heart, more clearly and abundantly displayed than in the letters he addressed to Madame de Montbéron. It was not without considerable hesitation that Fénelon consented to become, first her director and subsequently her confessor. He was loath to run the risk of involving so distinguished a lady—the Comte de Montbéron, her husband, was Governor of Cambrai—in the royal disfavour. But Madame de Montbéron, whose spiritual ambitions ran high, was not to be put off by apprehensions of the King's displeasure. Fénelon had been, as it were, the unofficial chaplain to that spiritual *Élite* (the ' Souls,' we might call them) at Court, which included among its adherents such illustrious women as the Duchesse de Beauvilliers, the Duchesse de Chevreuse, the Duchesse de Mortemart and Madame de Maintenon herself; and Madame de Montbéron, who aimed at nothing short of spiritual perfection, had long and eagerly looked forward to submitting herself to the guidance of so gifted and experienced a director.

If the pains which Fénelon took with his pupil are any indication of the measure of his esteem for her, he must have held her in very high regard. Yet it is easy to see that his patience was sometimes sorely tried.

Madame de Montbéron seems to have been a woman of somewhat abnormal sensibility, and to have been as morbidly anxious about her spiritual well-being as some women are about their bodily health. She was, it is hardly too much to say, a religious hypochondriac, a spiritual *malade imaginaire*. Realizing that this state of mind arises from an exaggerated egotism or self-centredness, Fénelon is continually exhorting her to fight against what he calls her *délicatesses*, her *scrupules*, that is to say her hyper-sensitiveness, her self-consciousness, or, in plain English, her ' vapours.'

Perhaps it had been better for Madame de Montbéron if she had sought guidance of someone less responsive, less sympathetic than Fénelon. Too much sympathy sometimes exaggerates the very evil it desires to allay. It might have been better for her peace of mind if she had gone with her interminable ' delicatesses ' to one who could not— or would not—understand them ; better if Fénelon —since she would betake herself to no one else— had encouraged her to increase rather than diminish that *oraison réglée*, the regular, set form of prayer, instead of laying such emphasis on the mystical contemplation of, and communion with, God. It may be that there was too much of the feminine in Fénelon's own spiritual constitution to make him an ideal physician to a soul tortured by that morbid over-anxiousness, that restless hyper-æsthesia which is a not uncommon malady among women, especially women of leisure. There are some subjective ailments which it is best to treat by seeming to ignore them. Women—and men, too, often enough —are like a child that has fallen and hurt himself. He restrains his tears till you begin to commiserate with him. But if Madame de Montbéron would have fared better with a less sensitive director, not only would the literature of religion have been immeasurably the poorer, but our knowledge of Fénelon himself, our insight into the heart and mind of that *âme d'élite* would have been infinitely less complete.

He urges her to study and to model herself upon St. Francis de Sales. We shall see why.

' The Feast of St. Francis de Sales,' he says, ' is a great festival for me, and to-day I am beseeching him with all the fervour I possess, to ask God to give you the same spirit with which he himself is filled. You will see, if you read his *Letters* and his *Life*, that he bore the highest honours and the bitterest rebuffs with the same unruffled calm and self-effacement. His artless, unaffected style reveals a lovable simplicity which surpasses all the graces and accomplishments one learns in the school of the world. In him you may behold a man who, though endowed with powers of penetration which enabled him to read deep in the human heart, nevertheless had no other desire or ambition than to offer such friendly counsel as might tend to console, to enlighten and to perfect his " even Christian." No one had attained to a higher pinnacle of spiritual perfection than he; yet to " the little ones " of this world he, too, was lowly, and never affected superiority in anything. He was all things to all men, not that he might curry favour with them, but that he might win them to Jesus Christ. There, Madame, you have the exemplar of the saintly spirit which I would fain see dwelling in you.'

It is the pattern to which he, too, would conform. ' To count the world as nothing,' he goes on, ' to feel neither pride nor mortification, is to live in the light of faith. Not to be unduly elated when things are in our favour, not to be unduly disheartened when they turn against us, but to bear good and evil fortune with a like equanimity ; to pursue our way in faith and trust, seeking, in all the multifarious activities of man, for God alone, who sometimes consoles us for our failings, and sometimes, in His mercy, visits us with tribulation—such is the true life of the children of God.' Of His *children*, be it observed ; that is, of those who love Him, not of those whose conduct is determined by fear of His retribution, who are slaves ; nor by those who order their ways in the expectation of reward, who are hirelings.

Madame de Montbéron seems to have been a kind of exquisite in her piety. Her virtue was not unalloyed with virtuosity and she had an eye to the opinion of the world. If her religious ardour was great, she was far from wishing to conceal it. So Fénelon thus admonishes her : ' If it is your wish that the Spirit of God should possess you, give ear no longer to the world.' And again : ' Be simple with Him who delights to communicate Himself to simple souls. Blessed are the poor in spirit.' From intellectual pride she seems not to have been wholly free : ' Oh, how I should rejoice,' he exclaims, ' if I saw you caring as little for intellectual attainments, as a penitent for bodily adornments.'

If it behoves us to be regular in our devotions, punctual in the performance of our religious obligations—prayer, fasting, going to confession, approaching the Sacraments—yet there are ' moments when God prefers to act by Himself alone, to keep the soul in silence, so that it may hear His most intimate communications. Nevertheless, at such times, the soul does not cease to play its part. It loves, it yields itself to grace. It behoves us to listen to the voice of the Bridegroom, to die to all worldly desires, to live to all the virtues with which the spirit of grace may inspire us according to our varying necessities. These acts—indefinite, even confused

L

as they may seem—contain the germs of every particular virtue called forth by occasions as they arrive. Do not, then, hesitate to obey the inward summons that may come to you in those moments of silence and meditation. Such moments do not occupy the whole of life. There will be abundant opportunity for you to turn again to the ordinary routine of religious observance.'

The silence of the soul, the Voice of the Bridegroom, the inward summons—what does he mean ? Is he thinking of that experience, of that fleeting enlightenment of those moments of strange, unaccountable insight which may visit the poet in his moments of purest inspiration no less than the religious devotee ? Is he thinking of that ' gift ' of which a later poet sings, of

> that blessed mood,
> In which the burthen of the mystery,
> In which the heavy and the weary weight
> Of all this unintelligible world,
> Is lightened : that serene and blessed mood,
> In which the affections gently lead us on,
> Until, the breath of this corporeal frame,
> And even the motion of our human blood
> Almost suspended, we are laid asleep
> In body, and become a living soul ?

These communings of the spirit with God—how can we describe them ? In what words shall we report them to the uninitiate ? When the mystics essay to put their experiences into words, too often they use language that bewilders or offends, language that sounds ludicrous or even blasphemous, the unintelligible or incoherent ravings of a disordered mind.

' When,' says Fénelon to Mme de Montbéron, ' we feel things which others do not feel, and which we have not (hitherto) felt ourselves, we are drawn to express ourselves as best we can and nearly always we find that in so doing we can but reveal half our meaning. If the Church finds that we do not express ourselves correctly, then we are ready freely to submit to her correction. Docility and simplicity are then our portion.' Bossuet himself ought to have been satisfied with such submissiveness. But it seems that, so far as Madame Guyon was concerned, even that capitulation was not enough.

Practical rules, by no means onerous or narrow, are plentiful in these letters. Here is an example of his psychological discernment. It concerns the difference between *courage*, and what he calls *bonne volonté*, which does not mean merely what we call goodwill. There is a bravery, a courage, that is vocal. It needs an audience. It proclaims itself to the world. It announces its intentions—saying very decisively what it will, and what it will not do.

> Under the bludgeonings of chance
> My head is bloody but unbow'd,

it will say. Or again,

> I am the master of my fate
> I am the captain of my soul.

And, really, this is not strength, nor a sign of strength, but weakness. Probably no man is less the captain of his soul than the man who boasts *urbi et orbi* that he is so. The brave man, the really strong man does not thus strike an attitude, or indulge in heroics. If you are going to set yourself to some task, some enterprise ' that hath a stomach in it,' or to some line of action that is going to involve struggle and sacrifice, it is well not to talk of it beforehand. It takes away some of the driving force. There was more strength in Charles Lamb, who never knew he was a hero, than in fifty self-proclaimed ' Captains of their souls.' He did not tell the world in advance what he was going to do, but somehow, not looking too far ahead, but going along quietly from day to day, doing 'the next thing', whatever it might be, *spatio brevi spem longam resecans*, nor asking to see the distant scene,

> Glad hearts, without reproach or blot,
> Who do thy work, and know it not.

Fénelon speaks of ' souls whom God wishes to keep lowly and whom he wishes to leave with nothing but the feeling of their own weakness, doing all that they are called upon to do without realising that they have it in them to do it, and without undertaking to go through with it. They themselves feel as if everything were conquering them, yet they conquer everything by means of something they have in them without knowing it, as though it were borrowed for the occasion, and which they never think of as belonging to them. . . . There is nothing striking, no outward indication of strength, to distinguish them in the eyes of others, least of all in their own. If you were to tell such a one that he had borne himself bravely, he would not understand you. He does not know, himself, how it came to pass. . . . Such is "goodwill," which seems to be less, but is in reality far more, than what is commonly called courage. . . . Goodwill is nothing more nor less than love of God's will. It has no colour nor brilliance of its own, it is only, on every occasion, what it has to be in order to will what God wills. Happy are they who already have some beginning, a seed, or germ, of so great a possession ! '

It must be, nevertheless, a difficult thing to direct others and to preserve our own humility, difficult to preach humility to one's neighbour, and oneself

remain humble.   Example is better than precept.
Fénelon set the example.   He was humble.   But his
humility had more of grandeur, more of majesty in
it than the tinsel splendours that shed their transient
glory on the Court of the Roi Soleil.

CHAPTER XV

THE FALSE DAWN

IN May 1711 the Grand Dauphin died, and the Duc de Bourgogne became the direct heir to the throne. Only the life of an old and perceptibly failing monarch stood between him and the crown. What manner of man was he whose accession to the greatest throne in Europe could not, in the normal course of things, be very long delayed ? As a child he had been quick-witted, violent-tempered, proud, wilful, yet at bottom upright, open-hearted, generous, and high-spirited. From 1695, when he was appointed to the Archbishopric of Cambrai, to 1697, when he was sent as an exile to his diocese, Fénelon had seen but little of his pupil, and after that, for four long years they had been cut off from every sort of intercourse, and not so much as a letter had passed between them. In 1701 they began to correspond again, and on two occasions they met face to face, although in the presence of witnesses, and great was the change that Fénelon noted. Instead of the lively, self-confident boy, so impatient of restraint, that he had known of old, behold a young man, shy, repressed, tongue-tied, and morbidly conscientious ! Fénelon felt that the process of taming this once wild creature had succeeded only too well and, it is said, he tried to undo the work he had done. But if the young man now showed himself almost too docile, too malleable, if he seemed cowed and almost afraid of his own shadow, was it Fénelon who was to

LOUIS XIV

blame ? Whatever the results that might have been
looked for from his teaching, excessive introspection
and an unhealthy anxiety about the *minutiae* of his
moral behaviour were certainly not among them.
No one was more impatient than he of over-scrupu-
lousness and the tendency to fuss about trifles, and
against this habit of mind he was forever putting
his penitents on their guard.

Disliked hitherto, or at any rate ignored, by the
King ; hated by his own father, whose vices,
stupidity, and folly were only brought out into
stronger relief by the almost painfully correct
behaviour of his son, the Duc de Bourgogne had
found himself in anything but an enviable position.
No wonder then that he was cowed. But now, all
was changed. His father, the old Dauphin, was dead,
and he himself had become a personage of first-rate
importance in the kingdom. The old King was
visibly softening towards him. He began to recover
his former spirit and initiative. There were signs
that he would rise to the heights of the great position
that would soon be his. If he still retained the
humility which Fénelon had inculcated upon him
as one of the most desirable of the virtues, it seemed
evident that it would not be a servile or cringing
humility.

Meanwhile a great change was coming over the
fortunes of Fénelon himself. The exile of Cambrai
was no longer a person about whom it was prudent
to speak in an undertone, or, better still, to keep
silence altogether. Cambrai was no longer a place
to be avoided as though it were stricken with some
infectious disease. It was plain to all that the Duc
de Bourgogne was now in sight of the throne, and
it was equally plain that the power behind that
throne would be none other than Fénelon. He whom
it had so long been politic to ignore was now one to
court and conciliate. Therefore the courtiers who

had so long been sailing on one tack were standing
by all ready to ' go about.'

And Fénelon himself—how was it with him ?
What was his state of mind ? What hopes, what
dreams was he nourishing ? It seemed that, against
all expectation, those theories of good government
which he had adumbrated long ago in his *Télémaque*,
and which he had lately set down clearly and formally
in the record of conversations regarding the government of the nation which he had had with the Duc
de Chevreuse at Chaulnes, and which go by the name
of the *Tables de Chaulnes*, were now at long last
about to be put into practice. His star, which had
suffered so protracted an eclipse, was about to shine
forth again with a new and greater effulgence. The
Golden Age of which he had dreamed for his country,
an age of simplicity, of freedom, of goodwill, of
religion, in which the King should be the leader
indeed, but the shepherd, the father, the friend of
his people, in which ingrained abuses, inveterate
injustices, were to be eradicated and swept away,
in which old institutions, purified and freed from
all contaminating incrustations, should be revered
and jealously preserved—in short the kingdom of
Numa or of Évander—seemed to be coming to pass at
last. If the reforms he proposed were, on the one
hand, a Utopian dream of a return to some past age
which perhaps never existed, on the other hand,
because they aimed at bringing the people into the
government, making them sharers of its responsi-
bilities, they were prophetic of the future, and, in
some of the measures he had in mind, we may detect
the seeds of what was to take place in 1789.

These then were his dreams and they seemed on
the point of coming to pass. The cloud was to be
lifted from him for ever. It was like the phantom
of false morning of which the Persian poet speaks.
Or like that delusive note of joy and triumph in a

Greek Tragedy when all troubles seem lifted, all perplexities resolved, all strife appeased, and we know that this is but the prelude to the climax, that the final and irremediable catastrophe is at hand.

On February 12, 1712 the Duchesse de Bourgogne died ; a week later the Dauphin followed her to the grave, and in that grave all Fénelon's hopes were laid for ever. That was the end.

' Alas ! ' he writes to the Duc de Chevreuse, ' God has bereft us of all our hopes for Church and State. He moulded this young prince ; He enriched him with gifts, and prepared him for his exalted station ; He showed him forth to the world, and lo ! in the twinkling of an eye, He has destroyed him. . . . There is but one thing now, and that is to give up all thoughts of the world, all thoughts of self, and to abandon our hearts unreservedly to the purposes of God. . . . Let us in very truth die to ourselves and to the world.'

The hour indeed was dark for his country. It was long since the fortunes of France had sunk to so desperate a level. Victory had forsaken her arms, destitution and discontent reigned among the people. The spectres of famine and disease were at her very door. The tide of war ebbed and flowed over Flanders. Cambrai was filled with wounded and fleeing men, refugees from all the country-side came crowding into the city, driving their flocks and herds before them. Fénelon turned his palace into a hospital and tended the wounded with his own hand. Nor did he make any difference between friend and foe. Such was his solicitude for the welfare of the enemy soldiers who had been wounded or taken prisoner that Prince Eugene and Marlborough gave stringent orders that the fields and granaries of the archiepiscopal estates should be religiously respected.

But in spite of all these excursions and alarms—or it may be by very reason of them—Fénelon's pen was

not idle. He busied himself with writing on a
diversity of themes. There was the second part of
his *Treatise on the Existence of God*, there was his
long controversy with the Jansenists, his *Manual of
Piety*, and various notes and reflections—*Mémoires*
he calls them—on political subjects, but of all these,
what is most interesting to us to-day, what is indeed
of perennial interest is the essay or series of essays
which has come down to us under the title of *Lettre
sur les Occupations de l'Académie*. To say that his
reputation as a humanist rests on this famous
production would be to say too much. His humanism
is implicit in all he ever said and wrote, it is as
inseparable from him as his own shadow ; nevertheless, this book, wholly concerned as it is with literature as a fine art, brings out and, as it were, incarnates
that tone or cast of mind which animates and
illumines his attitude, not only to Letters, but to
Life. It is, in a word, his literary *credo*, and it is
something more than that.

CHAPTER XVI

THE HUMANIST

FÉNELON'S life at Cambrai varied scarcely at all. The only event by which the daily routine would be diversified, or interrupted, would be a visit from one of his kinsmen, or a pastoral journey to some more or less distant part of his great diocese.

His day was a long one, for he woke early. Nevertheless, the extreme delicacy of his constitution made it necessary, or advisable, for him to remain in bed for some considerable time after waking. But there he was not idle. It was there that he said his office and his prayers, there that he read and replied to his letters, and issued directions on matters connected with dioccsan affairs.

As soon as he had risen and dressed he said Mass in his private chapel, except on Saturdays, when he said it in the Cathedral, afterwards hearing the confessions of all and sundry, like an ordinary parish priest. On feast days he officiated at the High Altar in solemn state.

At noon he sat down to dinner surrounded by the officers of his household, chaplains, secretaries, as well as visitors staying in the palace, and casual guests. Dinner over, he repaired with his entourage to the State Bedroom in which, as we have seen, he never slept. Here the company would talk at their ease, as at a sort of informal *conversazione* for about an hour, while Fénelon, seated at a small table a little withdrawn, signed his letters and official papers. In due course he retired to his study

where, if it were the winter season, he would remain till about half-past eight. Always, however, in the summer, and at other times if the weather permitted, he would go and pay a few courtesy calls in the city and visit the sick in the hospitals.

Supper was served at nine o'clock, a very simple repast consisting solely of eggs and vegetables. At ten o'clock the Archbishop read prayers in the presence of all beneath his roof, the servants included. Then he retired for the night. And so for him the days slipped

> slowly away
> One after one, to-morrow like to-day.

'The days are long,' he writes pathetically to one of his kinsmen, 'but oh, how brief the years!' *Eheu fugaces labuntur anni!* The tide of endless war swept by and through Cambrai, leaving, like a sort of *detritus*, the maimed and wounded in its wake. And the wounded he would tend with his own hand, caring for friend and foe alike with equal solicitude, whispering to each words of pity and loving consolation.

But it was not alone the wounded and the common soldiers that the war brought to his neighbourhood. 'For three or four years,' he once wrote, 'I have been seeing the Army here, and a large proportion of the Court. At the hands of these latter, I received innumerable marks of civility. Nevertheless, I am infinitely relieved to think that I shall not behold them again.'

There is a ray that illumines the figure of Fénelon the like of which shines on none other of that vanished world, however brilliant, however glorious in their day, not even on The Eagle of Meaux, no, not on *Le Roi Soleil* himself. How aptly apply those words addressed by an English poet of a later day to one who, in his grave humility, his sweetness and dignity and charm, was surely of one spiritual kindred

with the great exile of Cambrai—how fittingly, in
writing of Fénelon, we may echo the words in which
Tennyson greeted the shade of Virgil, that *anima
naturaliter Christiana*, and, looking backward down
the aisles of time, hail him with love and reverence,
and cry again :

> Light among the vanished ages,
>   Star that gildest yet this phantom shore,
> Golden branch amid the shadows,
>   Kings and realms that pass arise no more !

The Fénelon of those days of exile has been
exquisitely portrayed for us, as in an etching of
infinite delicacy, by Walter Pater in his ' Imaginary
Portrait ' of Antony Watteau. In the summer of
1714, the 'Prince of Court Painters' as he has come to
be known, arrived from Paris on a visit to his
kinsfolk at Valenciennes. His stay has drawn to a
close. Next day he is to return once more to the
scene of his triumphs, to Paris.

' On the last day of Antony Watteau's visit,'
writes Pater's imaginary diarist, ' we made a party
to Cambrai. We entered the cathedral church : it
was the hour of Vespers, and it happened that
Monseigneur le Prince de Cambrai, the author of
Télémaque, was in his place in the choir. He appears
to be of great age, assists but rarely at the offices of
religion, and is never to be seen in Paris ; and Antony
had much desired to behold him. Certainly it was
worth while to have come so far only to see him, and
hear him give his pontifical blessing, in a voice feeble
but of infinite sweetness, and with an inexpressibly
graceful movement of the hands. A veritable
grand seigneur ! His refined old age, the impress
of genius and honours, even his disappointments,
concur with natural graces to make him seem too
distinguished (a fitter word fails me) for this world.
Omnia vanitas ! he seems to say, yet with a profound

resignation, which makes the things we are most of us so fondly occupied with look petty enough. *Omnia vanitas !* Is that indeed the proper comment on our lives, coming, as it does in this case, from one who might have made his own all that life has to bestow ? Yet he was never to be seen at court, and has lived here almost as an exile. Was our " Great King Lewis " jealous of a true *grand seigneur* or *grand monarque* by natural gift and the favour of heaven, that he could not endure his presence ? '

His profound resignation ! ' Old age is stealing insensibly upon me,' he writes ; ' I know it and I am adapting myself to its demands, yet not altogether relaxing my hold on life. When I come to survey myself, I feel like a man in a dream, as though I were contemplating some figure in a Shadow Show. I no longer care for contact with the world. I am conscious of a barrier betwixt it and me, which banishes all my desire for it and which, I fancy, would cause me some embarrassment if ever I were required to mingle with the world again. . . . God gives us a strange book to scan when He bids us read our own hearts. I have within me a whole diocese, more onerous than the one without, and quite beyond my skill to mould anew.'

Thus wrote Fénelon of himself. In a beautiful phrase, M. de Broglie recalls St. Mary Magdalen's box of spikenard which, being broken, shed around it all the perfumes it had so long held captive. Fénelon's heart, he says, was like that. It broke slowly, slowly, under the pressure of reiterated grief, and, at last, all the air about him was filled with a mystic fragrance. His profound resignation ! Yes ; but every now and then the world which has borne so cruelly upon him wrings from his spirit, usually so serene, indeed so cheerful, a sigh, a moan of something like despair. As thus : ' Life seems to me like an indifferent comedy on which, in a brief hour or

two, the curtain will ring down. I hold myself even cheaper than I hold the world.' But these dark moods were rare, and as transient as they were rare. There was his faith, there was the Sanctuary in which the outer world was powerless to penetrate. His religion, his mysticism were his sure shield. But there were other things, though on a lower plane than these.

It is a strange thing how, when a man is beset with troubles, when he knows not, and hardly dares imagine, what further trials the future holds in store for him, he can yet turn aside from his anxieties and find solace, and an occasion for self-forgetfulness, in the pursuit of some familiar and absorbing study. ' Keeping the mind occupied' is a charm that rarely fails to dislodge that grim pillion-rider Care, let him haunt us never so persistently. Who, for example, would divine, if he had not been told, that those immortal pages of Newman, so limpid, so serene, which are gathered together in the volume entitled *The Idea of a University*, were penned at a time when anxieties were thronging, wave upon wave, and vainly spending themselves, against the invulnerable fortress of his spirit. So it was with Fénelon. By the death of the Duc de Bourgogne, his last hope of playing that part in his country's affairs for which his gifts of heart and mind befitted him, had vanished irrevocably away. That recon- ciliation with the ageing King for which he yearned so ardently, not indeed from any motive of secular ambition, but because he longed to be at peace with all men, was—he knew it in his heart—never, at least on this side of the grave, to be brought to pass. ' The Spring had been taken out of his year,' and it would never bloom again. Nevertheless, it was now, when his physical strength, always so frail and vacillating, was visibly declining, that his spirit revived and glowed for a while with a radiance

which to this day shines on undimmed by time. It was now that he produced a work which all lovers of Humane Letters will never cease to treasure as a jewel.

Whatever opinions may be held regarding the rights and wrongs of the great religious controversy which marked the crisis of his life, and in which, if he erred at all, he erred from generosity and chivalry of soul, none will deny that as a humanist he stands in the foremost ranks of his own and any other time. In delicacy of perception, in penetration, in the *justesse*, in the moderation and liberality of his literary judgements, he is unsurpassed, and unsurpassable. His sweet-reasonableness, his high-seriousness are such that, even when we differ from his judgement, we may yet gain from him a lesson in a thing whereof this present age stands in urgent need, that is to say, in *taste*. For those who have ears to hear and eyes to see, this taste of his—taste being an innate quality of heart and mind and soul mysteriously interfused—is betrayed even in his slightest acts, his most trivial utterances, but nowhere, at least so far as Humane Letters are concerned, is it more engagingly exhibited than in the famous pamphlet, for it is little more, which has come to be known as the ' Letter to the Academy.'

It was in the year 1695 that Fénelon was consecrated Archbishop of Cambrai ; two years earlier he had been elected to the seat in the Academy rendered vacant by the death of Pelisson, and thus he had been brought into more or less intimate contact with the leading figures in the literary world —and how numerous and brilliant were they !—of his era.

Towards the end of the year 1712, the Abbé de Saint-Pierre, the same Abbé whom Montesquieu was one day to hail as his ' master,' and whose independence of expression was in a few years destined to

bring about his expulsion from the Academy in which he now played a busy part, submitted to his brother Immortals, a syllabus, or scheme of work, for their approval. In this proposed plan he particularly emphasized the need for three things, namely, a Grammar, a Treatise on Poetry and a Treatise on Rhetoric. The Academy thereupon decided that all its members should be individually consulted in the matter, and that each should be invited to send in his comments on the present syllabus or, if he so desired, submit an alternative scheme of his own.

Fénelon's reply arrived towards the end of May, 1714. It was regarded by his colleagues as a delightful piece of work, but not conspicuously practical. ' Full of lofty, delicate and well thought out ideas,' said the Abbé de Saint-Pierre, ' it is expressed in terms of gracious elegance, well calculated to charm and instruct.' ' But,' he added, ' it leaves us as much in the dark as ever as to the work to which we should set our hands. We have to decide *what* to do ; not, at the present stage, *how* to do it.'

Fénelon's reply, which, fortunately for posterity, was not the arid, matter-of-fact document that was no doubt expected, was addressed to Dacier, the Academy's secretary.

' I am ashamed, my dear Sir,' it begins, ' to have kept you so long without an answer, but I must plead my poor health and a constant succession of worrying preoccupations as my excuse for the delay. Your appointment as perpetual secretary does honour to the Academy, and is rich in promise for all lovers of *belles-lettres*. I must confess, however, that the request which you have put before me in the name of an Association to which I owe so much, causes me a certain measure of embarrassment. Nevertheless, since I have been called upon, I will set down my ideas just as they come into my head. I

M

shall do so with a lively sense of my shortcomings,
and with unfeigned respect for those who have done
me the honour to consult me.'

First of all he makes mention of the Dictionary on
which the Academy were then engaged, evidently a
second and revised edition, as the first had appeared
as long ago as 1694. It must, he says, assuredly be
completed, although usage in living languages is
undergoing constant change, so that many of the
Academy's rulings are bound to need modification
sooner or later. And he quotes four well-known
lines from Horace's *Ars Poetica* :

> Nedum sermonum stet honos et gratia vivax.
> Multa renascentur quae jam cecidere, cadentque
> Quae nunc sunt in honore vocabula, si volet usus,
> Quem penes arbitrium est et jus et norma loquendi.

' The dictionary, of course, will be a *sine qua non* for
foreigners who may wish to read the various great
masterpieces in our tongue ; and it will also be
invaluable to such of our own people as may occasionally be in doubt regarding the strict and precise
connotation of a word. But, above all, when our
language has changed, how valuable it will be in
helping future generations to read and comprehend
those outstanding works of our day that are worthy
of the study of posterity. . . . What a delightful
thing it would be if we possessed Greek and Latin
dictionaries as used by the ancients themselves ! '

Among the works which, in obedience to its
charter, the Academy was required to produce was a
French grammar. A grammar had in fact been
compiled by the Abbé Régnier-Desmarais and had
appeared in 1708. It seems to have satisfied no
one, and Fénelon, we gather, was unaware of its
existence, for he says :

' It would be highly desirable that the dictionary

should be supplemented by a grammar. Foreigners studying our language and often bewildered by its irregularities, would find it an immense boon. French is our native tongue and we are so used to speaking it that we do not make sufficient allowance for a foreigner's perplexities. More than that, French people themselves might profitably have recourse to grammatical rules. They acquire the language by using it, but you cannot trust to usage alone. In every part of the country you find errors peculiar to the district. Every province has its incorrect modes of speech. Paris itself is not exempt.'

There follows an admirable warning to the learned against displaying too much learning. 'A learned grammarian,' says Fénelon, ' is in danger of producing a grammar with too many complications, too many rules. In my view, the method to be adopted should be quite simple and direct. To begin with, at any rate, let the compiler make his rules as general as possible ; exceptions can be dealt with, one by one, as they arise.' Example first and rule afterwards ; in other words the ' direct ' method. A grammar, Fénelon observes, cannot stereotype or crystallize a living language, but it may impose a check on those caprices of fashion which tyrannise over language as much as they do over the cut of people's clothes.

Coming to the language itself, as distinct from the rules which govern its correct use, he says : ' It is not without some trepidation that I venture to put before so learned a Society the proposition which follows : There are a number of words and phrases in which our language is lacking ; indeed it seems to me that for the past hundred years or so it has been notably impoverished by certain people whose aim has been to purify it. I do not deny that it may have been somewhat rugged, somewhat lacking in

organic form, somewhat redundant. Still, when we
read the work of old writers like Marot, Amyot or
Cardinal d'Ossat, we cannot help feeling a considerable measure of regret that their style of writing has
fallen into desuetude. Whether their theme was
grave or gay, there was a conciseness, an artlessness,
a boldness and a glow about them that we do not
meet with nowadays. If I am not mistaken, more
words have been taken from the language than have
been put into it. For my part, I would add new
ones without parting with any of the old.' ' Look,'
he goes on, ' how freely the Greeks introduced
compound words into their language, such as
pantokrator, glaukopis, euknemides. The Romans did
the same thing, but more sparingly ; for example,
lanifica, malesuada, pomifer. This process made at
once for brevity and magnificence. And where we
lack words, why should we not borrow from the
foreigner ? Thus the Romans did, and thus the
English do—without stint. What, after all, are
words ? Mere arbitrary sounds or symbols by which
we communicate our thoughts. There is nothing
sacrosanct about them. Why not freely add to our
stock such as we need, wherever we can conveniently
find them ? '

A dangerous doctrine that, against which he
himself enters a *caveat.* ' I confess,' he says, ' that
if we are in too much of a hurry to stuff our language
with borrowed words we shall but make it an amor-
phous congeries of other languages quite alien in
their genius to our own.' Perhaps, after all, his
fears were groundless. Language is no doubt made
for man, but it is made by a long natural process, not
by academies, not even by dictators, though some
have not been afraid to make the attempt. The
growth of a language resembles the growth of a tree.
It puts forth new shoots which the pruner, in the
shape of an academy, or the body of educated

public opinion may, in their wisdom, cut away or
permit to grow. But even the academy has often to
give way in the long run, and finds itself compelled
to permit, or at least to countenance, what it formerly
uncompromisingly condemned. As for the ingrafting
of something new, that is a much more ticklish
process and, even where it succeeds, the result is
generally, not so much an enrichment of the language
as an addition to its jargon.

And now as to Rhetoric. He begins by protesting
that he holds no brief for the Ancients against the
Moderns. He quite approves of the comparison
between a man and a fruit tree which, it appears,
had been adduced by the partisans of the Moderns.
Trees bring forth the same fruit as they bore two
thousand years ago, and man brings forth the same
ideas. Fénelon assents, but he takes leave to point
out two things. First, as some climates are more
favourable than others to the production of certain
kinds of fruit, so it is with the talents. For example,
Languedoc and Provence produce grapes and figs
far more delicate in flavour than those which grow
in Normandy and the Low Countries. Similarly,
the Arcadians were more adapted by nature to the
cultivation of the fine-arts than were the Scythians.
Again, music flourishes more readily in Sicily than
in Lapland. The Athenians were possessed of a
quicker and a subtler intelligence than the Bœotians.
The second thing to which he draws attention is the
long tradition of the power of eloquence which the
Greeks had behind them. With the Greeks, political
power lay with the people, but the people were
swayed by the spoken word. From Diodorus
Siculus he quotes the example of two orators who,
one after the other, moved the Syracusans to adopt
one resolution and then immediately afterwards
to exchange it for one diametrically opposite. One
persuaded them to spare the lives of the Athenian

prisoners ; the other determined them to put those prisoners to the sword. Fénelon points out that rhetoric has no such place in France. There, public assemblies were mere ceremonies and spectacles. No deathless examples of parliamentary eloquence had been handed down from generation to generation. The power of oratory was therefore infinitely less important in France than it was in Greece. Rhetoric played no part in the government of the country ; it was confined for the most part to the Law Courts and to the pulpit. A French advocate could scarcely be expected to exhibit the same ardour in striving to win a case for a private client as animated a Greek political orator when he aimed at possessing himself of the supreme authority in the State. An advocate does not incur the risk of personal loss. He receives his fee, whatever the verdict. If he is a young man, he strives to win a name for himself by pleading with all the eloquence he can muster. His name once made, he retires from the courts, because he finds readier and more plentiful remuneration in chamber-practice. The advocates most highly thought of are, not the most eloquent, but the clear reasoners, who can master the facts and have the law that bears upon them at their fingers' ends. But where are they who have the power of swaying vast audiences by the magic of their words and of stirring the heart of a whole nation ?

' Dare I venture,' he says, ' to criticize our religious preachers with equal freedom ? God knows how deeply I revere the preachers of His Word : but I shall wound the feelings of no individual among them if I remark in general that they do not all display equal humility, equal detachment. Young men, quite unknown, possessed of no authority whatever, rush into the pulpit. And the people whom they address not unnaturally come to the conclusion that it is less God's glory that they

have in mind than their own reputation. Their
speech is more appropriate to a showy orator than
to a minister of Jesus Christ and a dispenser of His
mystery. It was not with such ostentatious eloquence
that St. Peter preached Christ crucified in sermons
which changed the hearts of multitudes.' 'The
more,' he goes on, ' a speaker tries to dazzle me with
the skill and brilliance of his discourse, the more I am
repelled by his vanity. That man is alone worthy to
be heard who uses words for no other purpose than
to body forth what is in his mind, which should
ever be truth and righteousness. There is nothing
more contemptible than a professional phrase-
monger who displays his tricks of oratory as a
mountebank displays his nostrums.'

But Fénelon's whole doctrine of true eloquence,
as distinguished from self-conscious forensic display,
is summed up and, as it were, crystallised, in an
exquisite comparison he makes between Demosthenes
and Cicero. ' I protest,' he says, ' that I yield to
no one in my admiration for Cicero. He adorns
everything he touches. He makes words do what
no one else can make them do. He has, I know not
how many oratorical resources at his command. He
can be brief and vehement whenever it pleases him,
as against Catiline, against Verres, against Antony.
Nevertheless, we are conscious of something studied
in his discourse. His art is marvellous, but it does
not quite elude us. When he is thinking of the
safety of his country, he does not forget himself,
or suffer us to forget him. But Demosthenes seems
veritably to come out of himself. He sees his country
and nothing but his country. He makes no attempt
at rhetorical display. He is eloquent without thinking about it. He is above seeking for applause. He
regards words as a gentleman regards clothes, as
being, not for adornment, but for use. We cannot
criticise what he says, because he carries us away.

Our attention is wholly upon what he says, not on his manner of saying it. Both these orators delight me ; but I confess that Cicero, for all his inspired art and splendid eloquence, moves me less than the swift simplicity of Demosthenes.'

A true orator, according to Fénelon, brings no other ornament to his discourse than luminous truths, noble sentiments clothed in terms adequate to the matter of which he is treating and to the audience to which he is expounding it. ' He thinks, he feels—and the right word follows inevitably. A man of strong and lofty spirit with a natural gift for speaking and the facility that is born of practice, should never fear that words will fail him, his slightest utterances will have something distinguished about them, a *cachet*, a hall-mark which the mere rhetorician will never be able to imitate.'

How strangely these opinions and definitions are echoed by Newman. ' The mere dealer in words,' says the latter, ' cares little or nothing for the subject which he is embellishing, but can paint and gild anything to order ; whereas the artist whom I am acknowledging has his great or rich vision before him, and his only aim is to bring out what he thinks, or what he feels, in a way adequate to the thing spoken of and appropriate to the speaker.' It is true that Newman is speaking of literature, but still what he here says is equally applicable to the written and the spoken word. It is no less so in the passage which follows. ' A great author . . . is not one who merely has a *copia verborum*, whether in prose or verse, and can, as it were, turn on at his will any number of splendid phrases and swelling sentences ; but he is one who has something to say and knows how to say it.' Our own literature exhibits many examples of rhetoricians, great rhetoricians it is true, but little besides. ' Beyond the apparent rhetorical truth of things,' says Matthew Arnold,

speaking of Macaulay, ' he could never penetrate ;
for their vital truth, for what the French call the
vraie vérité, he had absolutely no organ. . . .
Rhetoric so good as his excites and gives pleasure ;
but by pleasure alone you cannot permanently bind
men's spirits to you. Truth illuminates and gives
joy, and it is by the bond of joy, not of pleasure, that
men's spirits are indissolubly held.' Such, too, is
Fénelon's conviction, in illustration whereof he
quotes St. Augustine : ' We must on no account
imagine that a man has spoken grandly and sublimely
because his speech excited frequent applause. The
tawdriest oratorical devices can achieve successes
of that kind. But what is truly sublime often weighs
upon our hearts, robbing us even of the power of
speech ; it brings us to tears. When I was
endeavouring to persuade the people of Cæsarea in
Mauretania that they ought to abolish a combat of
citizens held regularly at a certain season of the year,
in which kinsfolk, brothers, fathers, children, divided
into two opposing groups, strove for days together
each to kill his adversary, I sought with all the eloquence at my command to prevail on them to
abandon so hideous a custom. I had, however, no
hopes of success so long as I heard their cheers ;
but I conceived hope when at length I beheld them
weeping. The plaudits showed me that I had
arrested their attention and that my discourse had
given them pleasure. Their tears told me that I
had changed their hearts.' ' If,' adds Fénelon, ' St.
Augustine had weakened his discourse with elaborate
flowers of oratory he would never have succeeded
in reforming the people of Hippo and Cæsarea.'
Nor is St. Francis de Sales any less emphatic on this
point : *Artificium summum erit, nullum habere
artificium. Inflammata sint verba, non clamoribus
gesticulationibusve immodicis, sed interiore affectione.
De corde plus quam de ore proficiscantur.*

Fénelon now turns to what is perhaps the most engaging part of his whole letter, to a consideration namely of the nature of Poetry, *à propos* of the treatise which the Academy had undertaken to produce on that subject. Some of the observations he now sets down he had included earlier in a letter to Houdart de la Motte. As the views he expresses therein throw a considerable light on his theory of Poetics as expressed in his Letter to the Academy, it will be not inappropriate to give some account of them here.

Antoine Houdart de la Motte, member of the *Académie Française*, and a friend of Fontenelle's, was a very brilliant and a very ' modern ' figure of the times, a kind of Osric of literature. He is the author of some *Fables* in verse which contain a good deal of wit and a plentiful lack of poetry. He also wrote a tragedy, *Inès de Castro*, which had a great, and some critics hold, a well-deserved success. He possessed, it seems, a great command of the technique of versification, but not a spark of poetry. When, therefore, he announced his intention of undertaking to translate the *Iliad* into French verse, Fénelon was beset with the darkest misgivings. His sophisticated brilliance, his virtuosity, his artificiality were ill-calculated indeed to produce a satisfactory rendering of the simple but noble poetry of Homer. Fénelon is therefore filled with the gravest forebodings. But with what exquisite urbanity he expresses them, veiling his criticism of the translator in a judgement of French poetry in general ! So light is Fénelon's irony that the victim of it never suspected that it was irony at all.

' I am told,' writes Fénelon, ' that you are about to give to the public a translation of Homer in French verse. I shall be charmed to see so great a poet speaking our language. I have no doubts as to the fidelity of your translation, or as to the splendours

which will adorn your versification. Our age will
owe you a debt of gratitude for making it acquainted
with the simplicity of an antique world, and with
the innocence with which the passions are portrayed
for us, as it were in a picture. The enterprise is
worthy of you, but as you are yourself capable of
producing an original work, I would rather have seen
you occupied with a new poem, in which you would
doubtless impart some valuable lessons and depict
some fine scenes to the world. I would rather have
beheld you as a new Homer, whom it would fall
to the task of future ages to translate, than as a
translator of the Homer we already know. You
see that I have big ideas about you. They are not
misplaced.'

In comparison with that, even Matthew Arnold's
dexterous handling of the refractory Francis
Newman, which seems to offer a veritable model for
a controversialist seeking to subdue an obstinate, if
very learned, adversary, looks almost heavy-handed.

However, Fénelon's attempt to dissuade his
correspondent from prosecuting his fell intention
was of no avail. He gulped down the praise and
pursued his task, sending Fénelon in due course a
copy of his ' abridged *Iliad*,' concerning which
J. B. Rousseau remarked that ' it was longer in the
abridgment than in the text.'

' I have just been reading you, my dear Sir,' says
Fénelon, ' with genuine admiration. The powerful
prepossession I entertain for the author of the new
Iliad put me on my guard against myself. I was
apprehensive lest my personal predilections should
influence me unduly. I therefore imposed upon
myself that rôle of the rigorous and strictly impartial
critic. I recognised that in this work you had struck
out quite a new line for yourself. Now let me tell
you with perfect frankness what my impressions
really were, and please bear in mind that what I

am about to say applies, not to you personally, but
to French poets and poetry in general. I observe
then, at the outset, that the metrical scheme of our
lyrical poetry, in which the rhymes are interwoven
as it were in a pattern, offers a variety, a grace and
a harmony which our heroic couplets are utterly
unable to rival. These latter weary the ear in the
long run with their monotonous regularity. Latin
can boast of an infinite variety of inversions and
cadences. French, on the other hand, hardly admits
of inversion at all. It regularly follows one unalter-
able sequence : first the subject, then the predicate,
and finally the object. Again, rhyme is a drawback
rather than an assistance. It leads to the employ-
ment of superfluous epithets, it often impedes the
free, onward movement of the verse, and results in
meaningless elaboration. By increasing the length,
it diminishes the force, of what is said. Often, it is
necessary to insert an otiose and vapid line merely
that it may act as a vehicle for an effective one to
follow.'

The anti-rhyme doctrine briefly set forth to la
Motte reappears with many amplifications in the
Letter to the Academy. He speaks of the *Book of
Job*, the *Song of Songs*, the *Psalms* as examples of the
sublimest poetry and, turning to the Pagans, he
refers to Orpheus, Amphion, Homer, Tyrtæus as
among the greatest benefactors of the human race.
The use of rhyme, in his view, is a sort of strait-
jacket compelling the poet to subject himself to all
manner of contortions and distortions in order to
conform with its requirements. How Fénelon would
have approved of these words of a poet of a later day
who sings thus, denouncing rhyme :

> Oh ! qui dira les torts de la rime ?
> Quel enfant sourd ou quel nègre fou
> Nous a forgé ce bijou d'un sou
> Qui sonne creux et faux sous la lime ?

Nor is that the only sentiment of the great symbolist of the nineteenth century that Fénelon would have endorsed, for it was Verlaine, who, warning us against 'purple patches' and 'fine writing,' conjured us to 'take eloquence and wring its neck.'

Still, Fénelon does not want to do away with rhyme altogether. He looks on it as a sort of necessary evil, necessary since, without it, there would be no French poetry at all. 'In our language,' he says, 'we have not that diversity of "longs and shorts" which regulates the scansion of Greek and Latin verse.' All he would do would be to relax as far as possible the rigidity of the rules in order to afford the poet greater liberty in the use of rhyme. This would give him greater freedom in expressing his meaning and lend greater depth and variety to the music of his verse.

Next, he comes to 'inversion,' which the ancients used with such wonderful effect, holding the reader's mind in suspense, in breathless expectation of the wonder to come. He quotes as an example the opening lines of the Eighth Eclogue :

Pastorum musam Damonis et Alphesiboei,
Immemor herbarum quos est mirata juvenca
Certantes, quorum stupefactae carmine lynces
Et mutata suos requierunt flumina cursus,
Damonis musam dicemus et Alphesiboei.

'Take away this inversion,' he says ; 'put back the words in their normal grammatical order, and the rhythm, the majesty, the grace, the harmony—all would be destroyed.'

But inversion must be used sparingly. With the best intentions in the world, Ronsard went too far in this direction. There must be no sacrifice of clearness, for clearness is an indispensable virtue. 'A writer should never leave us in doubt about his

meaning. Inventors of riddles are alone entitled to
that privilege. French poets are too prone to refine
upon their ideas. They are apt to become too subtle
by half. In the matter of ornamentation, they don't
quite know when to stop. They are too heavy-
handed with the seasoning.' Again Horace and the
Ars Poetica are laid under contribution :

> Vir bonus et prudens versus reprehendet inertes.
> Culpabit duros, incomptis allinet atrum
> Transverso calamo signum ; ambitiosa recidet
> Ornamenta ; parum claris lucem dare coget.

In poetry, as in architecture, there should be no
such thing as ornament for its own sake. Ornament
should be an integral part of the structure. It was a
doctrine on which Fénelon, who introduced it into his
Discours de Réception à l'Académie, loved to dwell.
It is a doctrine no less dear to the heart of Newman,
who condemns the bad critic as one who considers
'fine writing to be *an addition from without* to the
matter treated of—a sort of ornament superinduced,
or a luxury indulged in, by those who have time and
inclination for such vanities.' Such critics as these
' speak as if one man could do the thought, and
another the style.'

Fénelon goes to plead for naturalness in writers.
He has a wholesome dislike of professionalism, of
' superiority,' of anything that savours of the *métier*.
' I like,' he says, ' the sort of man who makes me
forget that he is an author, the man who puts himself
on my level, as if he were talking to me. I like him
to show me a husbandman who is anxious about
getting in the harvest, a shepherd who knows
nothing but his own village and his own flock, a
mother filled with tender solicitude for her little
one. I don't want to have to think about him and
how clever he is. I want him to make his shepherds
talk so that I can listen to them.

Despectus tibi sum, nec qui sim quaeris, Alexi ;
Quam dives pecoris nivei, quam lactis abundans.
Mille meae Siculis errant in montibus agnae ;
Lac mihi non aestate novum, non frigore, defit,
Canto quae solitus, si quando armenta vocabat,
Amphion Dircaeus in Actaeo Aracyntho.
Nec sum adeo informis ; nuper me in littore vidi,
Quum placidum ventis staret mare :

How much more pleasing, how much more gracious
is this rustic simplicity than the sophisticated
subtleties of some " clever " writers I could
name ! '

A man who makes me forget that he is an author.
So also Pascal : ' When we meet with a style that is
natural we are surprised and delighted. We expect
an author ; we find a *man*.'

From now onwards, Fénelon yields himself up to
the praise of Virgil and of Horace, but chiefly of
Virgil.

' If a poem is really to put on beauty, the author
must forget himself and allow me to forget him.
He must leave me completely free. Here, for
example, Virgil must disappear and let me imagine
this scene of loveliness :

Muscosi fontes, et somno mollior herba.

I must long to be wafted to this other region,

O mihi tum quam molliter ossa quiescant,
Vestra meos olim si fistula dicat amores !
Atque utinam ex vobis unus, vestrique fuissem
Aut custos gregis, aut maturae vinitor uvae !

Needs must I envy, too, the lot of those who dwell
in this other place that Horace so happily describes :

Qua pinus ingens albaque populus
Umbram hospitalem consociare amant
Ramis, et obliquo laborat
Lympha fugax trepidare rivo.

I would far rather let my thoughts linger on that
green shade, that sparkling rivulet than be importuned by some clever wit that will not give me time
to breathe. That is literary work whose charm is
never exhausted. Far from losing anything by being
read a second time, such writers lure us back to them
again and again. To read them is not like work ; it
is rather rest and recreation. Clever books, books
which display the author's virtuosity may impress
and dazzle us for a time ; but sooner or later the
novelty wears off. I have no hankering for the
recondite, the far-fetched, the marvellous, but for
beautiful, simple, familiar things. If the flowers we
brush with our feet as we walk through a meadow
are as lovely as those which adorn the stateliest of
gardens, I love them the more for their very lowliness.
I envy no man anything. The things that are beautiful would be none the less beautiful, none the less
precious if they were common to all the human race.
Nay, they would be dearer than ever. The sun's rays
are not less golden because they shed their light on
all mankind. I have seen a young prince, a child
of eight, weep tears of sorrow as he heard the music
of these lines :

> Ah ! miseram Eurydicen anima fugiente vocabat :
> Eurydicen toto referebant flumine ripae.

And can we read such lines as these unmoved :

> O mihi sola mei super Astyanactis imago !
> Sic oculos, sic ille manus, sic ora ferebat ;
> Et nunc aequali tecum pubesceret aevo.

Cleverness, ingenious turns of phrase, would jar
upon us in a speech so poignant. Here, grief alone
should speak.'

And so he goes on with his quotations : Eurydice
again, the murrain of cattle, the beautiful things of
the natural world, hills and streams, trees and
flowers, the lament of Philomela. And not Virgil

alone, but Horace, and even Catullus (though he blushes for his obscenities) are invoked to exemplify that *simplicité passionnée* which he so dearly loved.

But this *naïveté* which he praises so highly in Virgil, is in fact the result of the most consummate art. Joubert, speaking of Racine says : ' Of Racine, as of his ancients, the genius lay in taste. His elegance is perfect, but it is not supreme, like that of Virgil.' Matthew Arnold, commenting on that passage, observes : ' Indeed, there is something *supreme* in an elegance which exercises such a fascination as Virgil's does ; which makes one return to his poems again and again, long after one thinks one has done with them, which makes them one of those books that, to use Joubert's words, " lure the reader back to them, as the proverb says good wine lures back the wine-bibber." '

Virgil then, for all the *naïveté* so highly praised by Fénelon, is a consummate artist. So, too, is Newman, so is Fénelon himself, but so also is Voltaire, and there is no *naïveté* about Voltaire. What then is the difference between them ? Is it that, while Virgil and Newman and Fénelon never think of themselves, while they lose themselves in their art, Voltaire never really thinks of anything else. In the last analysis Voltaire is a *poseur*, a magnificent, an incomparable *poseur*, but still a *poseur*, eternally striking an attitude.

The section on poetry was followed by dissertations on Tragedy and Comedy in which the plea for naturalness, for an avoidance of the windy, the bombastic, the artificial, the showy, occurs again and again. And again he renews his attack on rhyme. ' The cramping rules,' he says, ' which govern French poetry often lead the best of our tragic poets to write lines overloaded with epithet for the sole purpose of securing a rhyme. The loftier the

N

characters that are represented, the loftier their passions, the greater the need to make them speak with a noble and vehement simplicity. When Romans, for example, are brought upon the stage they are often made to declaim in language far too elaborate, far too ornate. Their thoughts were certainly noble, but they expressed them with moderation. They were the ruling people, it is true, *populum late regem*, but they were as urbane in social intercourse as they were resolute in subjugating other nations which disputed their sovereignty.' All through this part of his letter, Fénelon's advice to the writers of Tragedy inevitably recalls to an English ear Hamlet's counsel to those who would enact it : ' In the very torrent, tempest, and, as I may say, whirlwind of passion, you must acquire and beget a temperance. . . . Be not too tame neither . . . o'erstep not the modesty of nature.'

For what he calls the *goût pur et exquis* of Terence, Fénelon, like Newman, had a deep admiration, praising the *naïveté inimitable* with which he narrates ' some natural sorrow, loss or pain.'

Then he goes on to make a concession to the Moderns. ' I confess that Molière is a great comic poet. I do not hesitate to say that, in his characterization, he sometimes goes deeper than Terence. He has a wider range. He has struck out along a new path. He is a powerful thinker, but a bad writer. He will use the most forced and unnatural sort of language for things which Terence would convey in a few words with the most tasteful simplicity. I like his prose better than his verse. *L'Avare*, for example, is better written than his metrical plays. He indulges in caricature to please the " groundlings " and the less intelligent members of his audience. But worst of all he makes vice look attractive and virtue absurdly grim and ridiculous.'

After discussing Tragedy and Comedy he proceeds to consider History and historians. ' Your true historian belongs to no time or country. The man whose learning is greater than his powers as an historian spares his readers no date, no superfluous detail, no fact however dry, no circumstance however irrelevant. He pursues his way regardless of his public. He thinks everybody ought to be as interested as he is in the pettifogging *minutiæ* on which he concentrates his insatiable curiosity. A good historian on the other hand disregards facts which, leading nowhere, only serve to clog and retard his narrative. Let such superstitious exactitude be left to compilers. There are many obscure facts to which we can do no more than assign a date and a name. For all the good they do us, we might as well be without them. Better an inaccurate historian like Froissart, who gets his details wrong but presents us with a living, breathing picture, than the sort of barren chronicler who will tell me that Charlemagne held a parliament at Ingelheim, that he afterwards left that place, went to fight the Saxons and came back to Aix-la-Chapelle. That teaches me nothing. It is merely the dry bones of history. Very different from Cæsar, whose narratives seem to Cicero like well-painted pictures hung in a good light. History such as that excites the attention of the reader, he glows with eager anticipation as he sees one event leading up to another, while the climax of the story seems to elude him as though for the express purpose of whetting his curiosity. And when the book is finished, when he has turned the last page, he looks backward like an observant traveller who, on reaching a mountain top, turns and lets his gaze linger with satisfaction on the road he has come and on all the notable places he has passed on the way. And then, a saying reported with zest, some trifling detail, something with a splash of colour in it, something that lights up a man's character for you and tells you what he really is, is worth pages of cold and conventional description. And beware of piling on ornament. Like Beauty, History unadorned's adorned the most. *Nihil est in historia pura et illustri brevitate dulcius.* What an historian most needs is what he most often lacks, and that is a thorough knowledge of the customs of the country whose history he is relating. Those customs are perpetually changing from one age to another. What could be more absurd than to portray Frenchmen of the days of Henri II in wigs and cravats, or men of our own times adorned with beards and ruffs ! What an ignoramus a man would reveal himself if he talked about the meals of Curius and Fabricius as if they bore any resemblance to the rich and elaborate banquets of a Lucullus or an Apicius. Then the historian must know all about the changes that have succeeded one another in the forms of the government of the country with which he is dealing. He must know about the origin of fiefs, the conditions of feudal tenure, the enfranchisement of the serfs, the growth of the communes, the establishment of a standing army and a multitude of other things.'

Such a view of history was a new and startling one in Fénelon's day, nor was it to be realized until long years afterwards by Michelet and Augustin Thierry.

The concluding part of this famous Letter is devoted to the eternal quarrel between the Ancients and the Moderns. It is a conflict which in our day has been going steadily in favour of the latter. Classical studies occupy an ever smaller and smaller place in our educational scheme, and if things go on at the present rate it will not be long before Latin and Greek are banished altogether.

We may easily divine from all that has preceded on which side Fénelon's predilections really lay. He was, as Lemaître says, ' *tout nourri d'antiquité classique.*' Yet, because his spirit is a liberal and independent one, because no one was ever less of a fanatic, he strove to be fair to both parties, to hold the balance true, and to weigh the arguments impartially between them. ' Let me say at once,' he begins, ' that I hope the Moderns will surpass the Ancients,' ' but,' we seem to hear him add in a half-audible aside, ' they are as yet a very long way from doing so.' ' Of course,' he goes on, with the inevitable quotation from Horace, ' it would be absurd to judge a work by its date as if, like wine, it became the better for keeping. Undoubtedly, if the spirit of rivalry led the Moderns to make light of the Ancients and to neglect to study them, that would be calamitous. Let them extract all that is lovely and exquisite in the works of the older writers, then let them try to surpass them in their own field. But the modern writer must be on his guard against over-estimating his achievement. He must not get puffed up because his friends tell him he is a genius. It would be well for him to remember Virgil who, when on his deathbed, wanted to burn his *Aeneid*. Whoever, like Virgil, has within him a sense of the ideal, of perfection, will know that that is a goal forever beyond his reach.'

' Of course,' Fénelon goes on, ' I am well aware that even the most perfect of ancient authors have their imperfections. Homer himself " sometimes nods." ' And then, very surprisingly, he declares that for his part he has never been able to see the use, much less the charm, of the Chorus in Greek Tragedy : It interrupts the action, its pronouncements are often vague and not seldom irrelevant. It is not an uncommon criticism even in our own day, but it is unexpected in a mystic like Fénelon, for the Chorus voices the ultimate comment of the impersonal and eternal on the finite and the particular ;

it is, as it were, an echo of the final verdict passed on
the ways of man.

' Where the Ancients are unquestionably inferior,
is in their ideas of morality and religion. But that,
in spite of this immeasurable disadvantage, they
should have produced works of such transcendent
beauty is the more to their credit.

' But let us beware of mean and pettifogging
criticism in our estimation of the great classical
writers. Your mediocre critic has no eye for the
sublime. He will dispute with you about the order
of a word in a sentence, or about some expression
that transgresses his rules of syntax, but he never
raises his eyes from these vermicular occupations to
take in the general plan and contemplate the power
and beauty of the whole. It would be much better
if he confined himself to questions of orthography
and punctuation, whether a comma should come here
or a note of interrogation there. I pity the writer
who falls into his hands—*Barbarus has segetes.*'
Then he reverts once more to the question of
extraneous ornament, justifying his condemnation of
it by an illustration drawn from architecture: ' The
inventors of the architecture we call Gothic no doubt
deemed that they had surpassed the architects of
Greece. Now, a Greek building has no ornament
which is merely there for the sake of ornament;
but the parts which are necessary to support it or
to cover it, such as column and cornice, become
ornamental from the very beauty of their proportions.
All is simple and restrained, there is nothing that
does not play a useful part, nothing redundant,
nothing fanciful, nothing designed merely for effect.
So beautifully and truly is everything proportioned,
one to another, that nothing appears over-large in
comparison with the rest, however spacious the
whole may be. Everything conforms to reason.
How different from this is the architecture known

as Gothic. There the architect rears aloft on slender
pillars a mighty vaulted roof that reaches to the
clouds. You would think it must fall, yet it has
endured for centuries. It is full of lights and rose-
windows and pointed pinnacles ; you would think
the stone had been cut like cardboard, everywhere
there is open tracery, everything is airy, unconfined.
Now, in the place of " architects," put " poets "
and " orators," and you will see how it comes about
that these latter think themselves better than the
ancients, and what little reason they have for their
belief.'

' Well,' he concludes, ' I don't wish to set myself
up for a judge. I only want to warn those who adorn
this present age of ours not to make light of those,
their ancient predecessors, whom so many successive
generations have loved and honoured. I do not
set up the ancients as flawless models ; I would not
rob anyone of the hope of outvying them. I should
like to see the moderns win by studying the works of
the ancients and afterwards surpassing them. But I
must not go beyond my depth. Far be it from me to
presume to decide between these combatants.
Perhaps I have gone too far already and displayed
more zeal than knowledge. Perhaps I have already
been too decided, though I was anxious to avoid
anything that would convict me of bias, for one side
or the other. But it is time to stop :

> Phoebus volentem proelia me loqui,
> Victas et urbes, increpuit lyra,
> Ne parva Tyrrhenum per aequor
> Vela darem.'

And so, without pronouncing his verdict, he
gracefully withdraws under cover of a quotation.
But in literature, as in life, we know a man by the
company he keeps. Let him show us the sort of
thing he reads, and it will be easy to tell, more or

less accurately, what manner of man he is. Better
still, let us give heed to what he quotes, for what a
man quotes he has not only read but got by heart,
and to our hearts we only admit the things we love.
Judging by that criterion, we need not long remain
in doubt concerning Fénelon. Whenever he has
need of a quotation to support a theory, or to illus-
trate an argument, it is nearly always a classical
author that he lays under contribution. An ingenious
and industrious scholar, M. Léon Beck, the learned
proviseur of the *Lycée Henri IV*, has been to the pains
of adding them up. There are, he tells us, seventy
of them, and out of that seventy only two are taken
from modern writers. When Fénelon wants to show
us what writing really is, it is Virgil he quotes, or
Horace, or Homer, or Sophocles, or Demosthenes.
Horace and Virgil are those with whom he most loves
to dwell. ' Woe,' he cries, ' Woe unto him who feels
not the charm of lines such as this :

> Fortunate senex, hic inter flumina nota . . .'

And these, from Horace, yearning for the peace and
solitude of his country home, where he may dip into
the old books he loves and dream to his heart's
content, move him, he tells us, nigh to tears :

> O rus, quando ego te aspiciam ? quandoque licebit
> Nunc veterum libris, nunc somno et inertibus horis
> Ducere sollicitae jucunda oblivia vitae ?

Yes, he loves them both, but Virgil, I think, comes
first in his affections. That is what we should
naturally expect.

> Sunt lacrimae rerum et mentem mortalia tangunt.

And who was ever more alive to ' the sense of tears in
mortal things ' than Fénelon ?

CHAPTER XVII

ILLNESS AND DEATH

AT the beginning of his Letter to the Academy,
Fénelon speaks of his continual *embarras*,
by which he means the never-ceasing claims
of his great diocese, as the cause of his tardy reply.
These were public matters ; but for years past his
strength had been sapped, and his spirit saddened, by
a succession of intimate sorrows. Besides the death,
in February, 1712, of the Duc de Bourgogne, his
dearest friends, those whose lives were interwoven
with the very fibre of his being, were taken from him
one after another. It was as long ago as November
1710 that death had claimed him who was perhaps
the dearest of them all, de Langeron, ' the greatest
comfort of my life, and the best helper God has
given me in the service of His Church.' From that
blow he never recovered, that wound never healed.
' I confess,' he wrote a little later on, when he had
grown calm again after the first crushing blow,
' that it was for myself I mourned in mourning a
friend who was the flower of my life and whose loss
I never cease to feel. Alas ! all is vanity, all save
that death-to-self which only grace can give.'

This wound was still fresh when a further sorrow,
hardly less poignant, fell upon him. Two years
afterwards, almost to the day, death removed the
Duc de Chevreuse. A letter to the widowed Duchess
throws a revealing light on the beauty of his spiritual
nature. ' Think not,' he says, ' that he is gone from
us, because we see him not ; he sees us still and loves

us and knows our needs. He has safely reached his haven, but he never ceases to pray for us who are still exposed to the perils of the deep. His voice speaks in the silence of our hearts bidding us tarry not, but hasten to join him where he is. A holy friendship only changes visible companionship for that of faith. It mourns, but amid its tears it finds comfort in the certain hope of rejoining the beloved ones in the home of truth, in the bosom of Love itself.' Two more years go by and then, on August 31, 1714, the Duc de Beauvilliers, the last of that inner circle of friends who had clung to him with more than brotherly affection and loyalty, was taken from him. They had not met since Fénelon left Versailles to pass into the shadow of his lasting exile, but the pain was no less keen. 'Our dearest friends,' he writes, 'are the cause of our bitterest sorrow. One could almost wish that all dear friends could wait for one another and die on the same day.' The pang of leave-taking, even when the parting was but for a time, always caused him distress. But to bid farewell for ever to those he loved was almost more than his soul could bear.

Yet all was not gloom or sorrow within these palace walls. Sometimes the solitude would be brightened by the presence of children, and childish laughter would awaken the echoes of the long corridors and lofty chambers of that stately home. Fénelon loved children, and children loved him. His nephews and his nephews' children had always been dear to him, and nothing delighted him more than to have them around him. 'Do not forget your promise,' he writes to the Duc de Chaulnes early in the last year of his life, 'to send me your little ones when the warm days come. I want your children to come round about Whitsuntide when I shall have got back again from my visitation. They won't be the least in my way and I shall be head-

FÉNELON

tutor over M. Gallet, and, depend upon it, you won't get any compliments out of me.' So in due course the children came. The Vidame d'Amiens, the elder boy, was nine, his brother, the Comte de Piquigny, seven. With them came a cousin, the Comte de Montfort, a boy of eleven, the future Cardinal Archbishop of Sens. ' I am delighted,' he writes to their father, ' to have them here ; they cheer me up and are not the least in my way. Even if I have to go on a visitation, they will be as much at home as if they were at Chaulnes. This house goes along its customary routine way. In any case, I should not be long away and I should be charmed to find them here on my return.'

That same year, when the autumn was flaming away and the trees in the high-walled garden, beneath whose shade the children had loved to play, had changed from green to gold, Fénelon, in his turn, went to seek a little rest from his labours at Chaulnes, where he was ever sure of a loving welcome. It was his last taste of earthly joy. A little before Christmas, as he was returning to Cambrai after a brief pastoral circuit, the carriage in which he was driving collided with a parapet, as it was crossing a bridge. Though one of the horses was killed, Fénelon himself escaped with a shaking. But his constitution, already so frail and worn, never recovered from the shock.

On January 1, 1715, the Feast of the Circumcision, Fénelon was seized with illness. For him, there was no mistaking the summons. That illness, he knew, was to be his last. For six days he lay dying ; on the seventh he entered into his rest. The story of those last hours has often been told : how, as he lay on his death-bed, he bade them read to him from St. Paul's Second Epistle to the Corinthians, begging them sometimes to repeat this passage or that again and again; how, at his own request, he was

carried from the little 'grey room,' in which he
habitually slept, into the great state bedchamber
with its crimson hangings, in order that he might
take leave of all who should wish to bid him farewell
ere he set forth on his last journey ; how, on the
fourth day of his illness, his nephews, the Abbé de
Beaumont and the Marquis de Fénelon arrived in
hot haste from Paris, having borrowed Saint-Simon's
travelling coach and the Duke of Orleans's physician
—the eminent Chirac—for the occasion, and how
they could not speak for weeping when their uncle,
who evinced great satisfaction at seeing them, en-
quired whence they had learned the tidings—all this
has been told, and how, towards the end, certain of
the townsfolk whom he had in various ways befriended, counselled and consoled, came to take
their leave of him and to ask his blessing. It has
been related, too, how his chaplain at his bidding
read him certain lines from the office of St. Martin,
and how, broken-hearted at the thought of losing so
dear a friend and master, the reader's voice faltered
as he came to the words : ' *O virum ineffabilem, nec
labore victum, nec morte vincendum, qui nec mori
timuit, nec vivere recusavit* '—O dear beyond words,
whom toil overcame not, nor death could conquer,
who feared not death, nor chafed against life—and
how he broke down completely at the words : ' *Cur
nos, Pater, deseris, aut cui nos desolatos relinquis?
Invadent enim gregem tuum lupi rapaces* '—Where-
fore, Father, dost thou forsake us, and to whom dost
thou leave us in our desolation ? For the ravening
wolves will invade thy flock.

On Epiphany morning, Fénelon being greatly
afflicted in spirit for that he could not say his
Mass, his chaplain, obedient to his wishes, went
to say it in his stead. During this brief interval
he grew rapidly weaker and was given Extreme
Unction.

Then he sent for his chaplain and having bidden everyone else depart, he summoned up all his remaining strength and dictated a letter which, when it was finished, he signed and gave orders that it should be dispatched as soon as his eyes were closed. It was addressed to Father Le Tellier, the King's chaplain. That night he suffered grievously. The fever, having worked its will upon the body, now laid siege to the mind, and many times he waxed delirious, wandering in his speech. Then he would grow calm again, and collect his thoughts, and address himself to prayer. In these intervals of consciousness, his kinsmen, the Abbé de Fénelon, the Marquis de Fénelon, the Abbé de Beaumont, the Chevalier de Fénelon and some others, his friends, came and knelt at his bedside, one after another, to receive his blessing. Afterwards, all his servants came and, weeping, begged that he would bless them also. This he did very sweetly. The Abbé Le Vayer, a member of the Congregation of Saint-Sulpice and Superior of the Seminary at Cambrai then recited the prayers for the dying, after which, lying for a space in perfect stillness, without giving any sign of consciousness, he died, quite peacefully, at a quarter past five in the morning of January 7, 1715.

Fénelon was laid to rest with great simplicity beneath the High Altar of his Cathedral Church of Cambrai. Of all the Archbishops of that place, he was the only one over whom no funeral panegyric was pronounced. It was feared that to do so would give umbrage to the King. Once more the wind had changed. The King gave no sign of relenting, nor did he show any mark of sympathy to the relatives of the dead prelate ; but Pope Clement is said to have wept on hearing of the death of so illustrious a son of the Church ; tears of sorrow at his own bereavement, tears of regret that, from motives of political prudence, he had never made a

Cardinal of one whom, in his heart, he had so
desired to honour.

In 1793 the Cathedral was destroyed and Fénelon's
tomb laid bare. It was generally given out that the
coffin was wrenched open, the remains flung to
the four winds and the leaden shell melted down for
bullets. This, it seems, was an exaggerated account
of the matter. The Revolutionaries, who were not
always so careless of their opportunities, must be
acquitted of this crowning infamy. At any rate,
official documents are extant purporting to show that
the remains were found by the Mayor of Cambrai.
The leaden coffin had been rudely forced open,
exposing a wooden shell within which were the
remains of the Archbishop. Close by, lay the
scattered fragments of a monumental stone which
when pieced together was found to bear the
inscription :

HIC JACET

FRANCISCUS DE SALIGNAC DE LA MOTHE DE FÉNELON

ARCHIEPISCOPUS CAMERACENSIS DEFUNCTUS DIE

SEPTIMA

JANUARII 1715 ; E PRIORI TUMULO TRANSLATUS

DIE 28 MARTII 1720

CHAPTER XVIII

CONCLUSION

EVEN for those who know Fénelon never so slightly, know perhaps only the barest circumstances of his life, there is an aureole of light about his figure, however vague and shadowy that figure itself may be. It is almost as if lives lived with such passionate spiritual intensity literally leave behind them a visible gleam, like that mysterious fire with which the Dioscuri tell the storm-tossed mariner that they have not forsaken him. 'A fugitive and gracious light,' not to be seen by all, yet a light which, once descried, kindles in the beholder an answering flame of unquenchable devotion. It is strange how this effect of light, as of a star amid the shadows, is called up by the mere mention of certain names, Virgil, for example, Newman and, again, Fénelon. It is not the suffused glory, the wide splendours of the risen sun or of high noon; that effulgence is Homeric, or Shakespearean. It is not a blaze, but a point of light, and it is not of the morning, but of the evening. *Stella vespertina!* It speaks of hope, indeed, but less of hope than of consolation.

Le plus bel esprit et le plus chimérique de mon royaume—so King Louis called him, King Louis, that eminently egoistic, practical, politically-minded sovereign who looked on those mere human beings, his subjects, as if they were pawns, and cared not a whit more what befel them individually than if he had been Olympian Jove himself. *Chimérique!* If that means, ' visionary,' ' Utopian,' there is perhaps

195

a modicum of truth in it. It were as easy to ensnare a moonbeam, or grasp the rainbow as to analyse, dissect and catalogue the elusive clements of a spirit so mobile, so Ariel-like as Fénelon's. But to seize on his most obvious, his least disputable characteristic, let us consider his love of, and insight into, Humane Letters. It is in the dual rôle of Educationist and Humanist that he exerts his greatest influence to-day. His Treatise on the Education of Girls, his Letter to the Academy are still read and studied far beyond the frontiers of their land of origin. *Il est humaniste avec délices*, says one of the acutest and most sympathetic of his critics, Jules Lemaître. *Il adore l'antiquité paienne ; il y veut trouver et il y goûte une simplicité riante et innocente, qu'il croit que la civilisation a altérée.'* For Virgil, as we have seen, Fénelon entertained a peculiar veneration and, though he praises him mainly for his love of the *nescia fallere vita*, and for his portrayal of the innocent and joyous simplicity of a somewhat idealised country existence, he cannot but have been strangely drawn by another quality, deeper far, more mysterious and more lovely still. Fénelon describes poetry as *peinture*, a portrayal or picture. The office of the poet, he maintains, is ' to hold the mirror up to nature.' But there is another element in all great verse, and particularly in Virgil, an element vaguer, hardly susceptible of definition, but more compelling, more profound : the element of music. ' What is meant,' says F. W. H. Myers in his incomparable essay on Virgil, ' by the vague praise so often bestowed on Virgil's unequalled style is practically this, that he has been, perhaps, more successful than any other poet in fusing together the expressed and the suggested emotion ; that he has discovered the hidden music which can give to every shade of feeling its distinction, its permanence, and its charm ; that his thoughts seem to come to us on the wings of melodies prepared for them from the foundation of the world.' He who wrote that—never surely did critic come nearer to defining the indefinable—was thinking of no pictures of country life, no pastoral scenes, however smiling, however fresh, however innocent. He was thinking of something different and deeper, he was thinking of the music, infinitely sweet and mournful, that sounds in such a line as :

> Tendebantque manus ripae ulterioris amore

or as :

> Sunt lacrimae rerum, et mentem mortalia tangunt.

For the like of that music, music whose solemn, stately *adagio* is echoed by no other poet ancient or modern, we must listen to the winds in autumnal forests, or to the sound of the wave that far away

> Doth seem to mourn and rave
> On alien shores.

It is, in truth, as Newman says, when he speaks of Virgil, ' giving utterance *as the voice of Nature herself* to that pain and weariness yet hope of better things which is the experience of her children in every time.' It must have been not only the singer of tilth and vineyard, hive and horse and herd that cast his spell upon Fénelon, but that *anima naturaliter Christiana*, whose memory is invoked in the following lines contained in a mediæval Mass :

> Ad Maronis mausoleum
> Ductus fudit super eum
>   Piae rorem lacrimae ;
> Quem te, inquit, redidissem
> Si te vivum invenissem,
>   Poetarum maxime.

The Virgil that we associate with Fénelon was he whom Dante had in mind when he spoke these

o

words : ' May the long zeal avail me and the great
love that made me search thy volume. Thou art my
master and my author. Thou art he from whom I
took the good style that did me honour.'

' In highly cultivated societies,' Myers remarks,
' there is a craving to escape from all that speaks of
effort and preparation, into the refreshing simplicity
of an earlier age. This craving was strongly felt
under the Roman Empire. . . .' It was no less
strongly felt under Louis XIV of France. It is
true that in the passage just quoted Myers is account-
ing for the tendency manifested by certain modern
critics, especially in Germany, to exalt Homer at
the expense of Virgil. But it is the desire to escape
from the pressure of a highly complex and artificial
mode of life that we are considering, and whether,
for that relief, we turn to Homer or to Virgil or to
both, does not affect the issue. In Homer and in
Virgil, particularly in the *Bucolics* and the *Georgics*,
Fénelon must have caught something of that austere
yet gracious simplicity of life made dear to him by
the memories of his own early days in his native
Périgord, the kind of scenes which were present to
his mind when, a life-long exile from the places that
inspired them, he tuned his lyre to such nostalgic
strains as these :

Bois, fontaines, gazons, rivages enchantés,
Quand est-ce que mes yeux reverront vos beautés
Au retour du printemps, jeunes et refleuries ?
Cruel sort qui me tient ! Que ne puis-je courir ?

Creux vallons, riantes prairies
Où de si douces rêveries
A mon coeur enivré venaient sans cesse offrir
Plaisirs purs et nouveaux qui ne pouvaient tarir !

Hélas que ces douceurs pour moi semblent taries !
Loin de vous je languis ; rien ne peut me guérir :
Mes espérances sont péries
Moi-même je me sens périr :

Collines hâtez-vous, hâtez-vous de fleurir.
Hâtez-vous, paraissez ; venez me secourir,
Montrez-vous à mes yeux, O compagnes chéries !
Puissé-je encore un jour vous revoir et mourir !

As for the long and bitter controversy that ended
in the condemnation of his book, we, who are able
to view the matter as a whole, calmly and dis-
passionately, can hardly question either the justice
or the wisdom of the sentence to which he was called
upon to submit, however much our sympathies and
affections may be drawn to the object of it.

There are minds and temperaments sensitive,
eager, generous, profoundly religious, which by their
passionate enthusiasm may be led quite involuntarily
to form ideas and to seek to disseminate them,
which, if their foresight were at all commensurate
with their zeal, they would have modified or
altogether abandoned. At first sight, and to their
own glowing imagination, their theories and doctrines
may seem fraught with nothing but good, and
opposition to them to be dictated by ignorance,
bigotry, or jealousy. But just as a line which,
in the limited section we are able to view of
it, seems perfectly straight, may, if prolonged,
discover an unsuspected curve or bias, so may a
seemingly innocent theory or doctrine contain
within it the seed of an intrinsic fault which, late or
soon, will bring it to disaster. It is not merely the
beginning, but the ulterior course, of the trajectory
that we must attempt to visualize. How often, in
the political sphere, have well-meaning and
apparently beneficent measures had to be withdrawn because they have proved, on experiment,
not only to have intensified the evils they were
designed to mitigate but, perhaps, to have engen-
dered new ones.

But there is another aspect of the matter to be considered. Madame Guyon, having found what she

deemed a treasure, generously desired to share it with
others. That ambition, praiseworthy and disinterested
as were the motives which inspired it, was her undoing. The Church includes all sorts and conditions of
men and women within her pale—saints and sinners,
learned and ignorant, gentle and simple, ingenuous
and sophisticated, rich and poor ; and to all these,
thus multifarious in their fortunes, character and
natural attributes, she must needs adapt her system.
Her wisdom is deeper, her arm longer, her vision
more penetrating than any of her children's. No
individual, however conspicuous his intellectual
gifts, however shining the aureole of his sanctity,
may presume to dictate to her the substance or the
manner of her teaching. Though she may, if she
thinks fit, acquiesce in, or even tacitly approve, a
certain attitude of mind in this individual or in that
as being appropriate to the special circumstances of
his case, she cannot tolerate that any individual
should usurp her functions by elevating his private
and personal notions into a system, and proclaiming
its applicability to Christendom as a whole.

There have not been wanting men who declare
that the Pope condemned Fénelon's book because
he was afraid to do otherwise. His decision is
represented, not as an independent judgement but as
a verdict extorted from him under duress. In short,
it is said that he would have pronounced in favour of
Fénelon had he not been bullied and brow-beaten
by Louis XIV and his agents into condemning him.
'That (in accepting his fate),' says one of his
biographers, ' he (Fénelon) was able to remain
steadfast to the Roman faith and its doctrine of
Papal infallibility, is a mystery difficult of solution ;
his reason told him that Innocent XII was false and

shifty, and that he had given judgement in a question
of belief against his reason, to curry favour with the
Court of France.' Fénelon, like Brutus, was an
honourable man, pure in heart, true and without
guile in all his dealings ; yet Fénelon ' remained
steadfast to the Roman faith.' How could this be ?
Now, let it be granted, for the sake of argument, that
all the charges so industriously brought forward
against Pope Innocent XII were well founded, it
must nevertheless be borne in mind that we are here
concerned, not with the circumstances in which the
verdict was delivered, but with the verdict itself.
The organ through which the decree was pronounced may have been worthy or base ; the decree
itself may have been dictated by policy, or extorted
by threats, or procured by intrigue, still, these
considerations, however interesting to the historian,
are irrelevant to the point at issue, which is, simply,
whether the decree was calculated to preserve the
Faith or to contribute to its disintegration. One
may be intensely attracted by the character and
personality of Fénelon himself—and if the charm
he still exerts on his remote posterity remains so
great, what must have been the spell he cast on
those who once came within the magic circle of his
presence ?—yet precisely because Fénelon exerts so
potent, so winning an influence on the hearts of all
of us who learn to know him through his writings,
it is all the more important for us to be on our guard
lest, for the mere love of him, we be tempted to
subscribe to a teaching, which, though conceived
and urged with irreproachable intentions, has proved
in the long run to be attended with serious dis-
abilities. A hair, they say, divides the false and true.
And a hair's breadth, which seems negligible enough
to-day, will, in the course of time, like the rift in
the lute, develop into a formidable fissure. Since
Voltaire and Rousseau both appear to have discerned

in Fénelon their spiritual and intellectual prototype,
and since Fénelon, ' by merit raised to that bad
eminence,' is the solitary ecclesiastic who appears
among the miscellaneous demi-gods whose busts
adorn the Pantheon, there seems after all to be at
least some *prima facie* ground for holding that the
verdict of Innocent XII, whatever the circumstances
that preceded it, has not been without its justification.
Though it is not here suggested—Heaven forbid !—
that Fénelon would ever have developed into a
Rousseau or a Voltaire, it is not impossible that his
teaching was expressed in such a manner as might,
with a little manipulation and distortion, provide a
handle to the enemies of that Faith which Fénelon
would have died rather than imperil.

As for Rousseau, of whom Fénelon is sometimes
regarded as the precursor, Bernardin de St. Pierre
once said to him : ' If Fénelon were alive to-day,
you would be a Catholic.' ' Oh ! if Fénelon were
alive,' replied Rousseau, in tears, ' I should try to
become his lackey in order to deserve to be
his valet.' ' The great and the noble,' says Janet,
' are the dominant elements in his life. The
Fénelonian legend, like all legends, springs from
the truth. He was, and still remains, the most
winning, the most enchanting figure of the
seventeenth century.'

INDEX

A

Abzac de la Douze, Marquis d', 4
Amiens, Bishop of, 118
Amiens, Vidame d', 191
Amyot, 168
Apicius, 184
Arnold, Matthew, 172, 175, 181
l'Astrée, 70
Augustine, St., 37, 38, 46, 63

B

Barre, Poulain de la, 42
Baumelle, M. de la, 118
Bausset, Cardinal de, 65, 138
Bayle, Pierre, 65
Beaumont, Abbé de, 130, 143, 145, 193
Beauvilliers, Duc de, 31, 32, 112, 190
Beauvilliers, Madame de, 41, 51, 133, 146
Beck, M. Léon, 188
Bergson, Henri, 33
Bossuet, Jacques Benigne, Bishop of Meaux, 2, 13, 16, 31, 32, 38, 39, 61, 69, 70, 71, 86, 91, 95, 108, 110–112, 114–122, 125–131, 133–137, 139, 142, 151, 160
Bossuet, Abbé, 121, 133, 134
Bouquier, 10, 11
Bourdaloue, Louis, 38, 39

Bourgogne, Duc de, 49, 51, 60 *et seq.*, 69, 73, 74, 79, 115, 154, 155, 157, 189
Bourgogne, Duchesse de, 157, 163
Bouteroue, 113, 114
Brancas, Duchesse de, 30
Bremond, Abbé Henri, 83, 84, 85, 86
Bretonvilliers, M. de, 114
Brian, Alexander, 58
Broglie, Em. de, 142, 162

C

Cæsar, Julius, 183
Calvin, Jean, 58, 110
Cambrai, the Archiepiscopal Palace at, 140 *et seq.*
Catullus, 181
Chantal, Mme de, 96, 138
Chanterac, Abbé de, 134, 135, 143, 144
Charlemagne, 183
Chartres, Bishop of, 107, 118
Chaulnes, Duc de, 190
Cherel, M., 86
Chevreuse, Duc de, 31, 32, 109, 112, 146, 156, 189
Chevreuse, Duchesse de, 189
Chirac, 192
Cicero, 171, 183
Clement XI, Pope, 193
Cranmer, Thomas, 58
Curius, 184

The Mayflower Press, Plymouth. William Brendon & Son, Ltd.